Radical Islam's War Against Israel, Christianity, and the West

Radical Islam's War Against Israel, Christianity, and the West

Dr. Richard Booker

 Unless otherwise identified, Scripture quotations are from *The New King James Bible Version.* © 1979, 1980, 1982, Thomas Nelson, Inc. Publishers. All English-language interpretations of the Koran are from *The Koran.* Translated by N.J. Dawood. Penguin Books USA, Inc. 375 Hudson Street, New York, New York 10014, USA, 1993. Please note that Destiny Image's publishing style capitalizes certain pronouns in Scripture that refer to the Father, Son, and Holy Spirit, and may differ from some publishers' styles. Take note that the name satan and related names are not capitalized. We choose not to acknowledge him, even to the point of violating grammatical rules.

DESTINY IMAGE® PUBLISHERS, INC.
P.O. Box 310, Shippensburg, PA 17257-0310

"Speaking to the Purposes of God for this Generation and for the Generations to Come."

This book and all other Destiny Image, Revival Press, Mercy Place, Fresh Bread, Destiny Image Fiction, and Treasure House books are available at Christian bookstores and distributors worldwide.

For a U.S. bookstore nearest you, call **1-800-722-6774**.
For more information on foreign distributors, call **717-532-3040**.
Reach us on the Internet: **www.destinyimage.com.**

ISBN 10: 0-7684-2594-8
ISBN 13: 978-0-7684-2594-9

This book contains excerpts from the following previously published booklets by Richard Booker: Why Christians Should Support Israel; The Time to Favor Zion has Come; The Battle for Truth: Middle East Myths and the Arab-Israeli Conflict; and Islam, Christianity and Israel.

For Worldwide Distribution, Printed in the U.S.A.
1 2 3 4 5 6 7 8 9 10 11 / 11 10 09 08

ACKNOWLEDGMENTS

Much of the information in this book is taken from the following booklets published by the author and used with his permission: *Islam, Christianity and Israel, The Battle for Truth: Middle East Myths and the Arab-Israel Conflict, The Time to Favor Zion,* and *Why Christians Should Support Israel.* In light of the challenging times in which we are living, it seemed prudent to put this important information into one book for easy reading and reference.

Table of Contents

Preface

After being scattered for almost two thousand years, the Jewish people are now being re-gathered to their ancient homeland, Israel. This is one of the most remarkable and significant happenings in history that is destined to change the world. And it is taking place right in front of our eyes.

This historic re-gathering of the Jewish people was predicted centuries ago in the pages of the Bible. In fact, if you are not knowledgeable of the Bible, or if you consider the Bible irrelevant, you simply cannot understand the daily news. Without an understanding of the biblical story of Abraham, Isaac, and Jacob, who was called Israel, you cannot possibly understand the modern miracle of the State of Israel and the Arab-Israeli conflict.

My friend, MK Rabbi Binyamin (Benny) Elon says that Israel is real, the Word of God is real, the covenant between God and Israel is real and the State of Israel is real. What Benny says is absolute truth. Unfortunately the nations of the world, led by Islamic hatred of Israel and the Jews, do not accept what is real. They do not accept the biblical story as being true and relevant for our times.

Islamic leaders deny the Holocaust ever happened and deny the biblical record of God's covenant with the Jews declaring that Islam has superseded both Judaism and Christianity. Furthermore, world leaders, who now say it is a crime to deny the Holocaust, ironically want to deny Israel's right to exist. Age-old Anti-Semitism is now disguised as anti-Zionism or anti-Israel.

It is important for Christians to understand that Esau's ancient hatred against Jacob is not limited to the Jewish people and the modern State of Israel. Muslims consider both Christians and Jews as "People of the Book." Their end-time theology teaches that both Jews and Christians will either convert to Islam or be killed and that Islam will rule the world. This belief is summarized in their cry of jihad, "Today we fight the Saturday people (the Jews) and tomorrow we fight the Sunday people (the Christians)."

It is imperative that Christians understand Islamic theology as it pertains to Christianity as well as to Jews and Israel. It is also critical that Christians and Jews rise above their own tragic past and work together to preserve our Judeo-Christian heritage and way of life. Our future and destiny depends on it.

This is why I have written this book. Specifically, I wrote it for the following reasons:

1. To awaken Christians and Jews to radical Islam's goal to conquer the world.
2. To give the reader a better understanding of Islam, Christianity and Israel.
3. To explain the truth behind the Arab-Israeli conflict.

4. To encourage the "People of the Book" that no matter how challenging the days ahead, the God of the Bible is a faithful covenant-keeping God.
5. To encourage Christians and Jews to stop fighting among themselves over past concerns that are now not important and stand together against the Haman's of this world "for such a time as this" (Esther 4:13).

INTRODUCTION

Where were you when...? The World War II generation of Americans asked this question about a sneak attack against America. It was December 7, 1941, when the Japanese attacked Pearl Harbor. President Roosevelt said it was a "day that would live in infamy." It was certainly a day that changed the world. My generation of Americans asked, "Where were you on November 22, 1963"? That was the day Lee Harvey Oswald shot President Kennedy in Dallas, Texas.

Now the younger generation, and all Americans ask, "Where were you on 9/11"? We all know what they mean by this question, and most of us can tell where we were and what we were doing when we heard the news about radical Islamic terrorists hijacking planes and crashing them into the World Trade Center buildings. And while our government has made some changes regarding the security of our country, most Americans believe another attack is coming. It is not a matter of if, but when!

AMERICA UNDER ATTACK

The radical Islamic threat to Israel and the Middle East has finally come to America. On February 26, 1993, Islamic Palestinian militants associated with the Hamas terrorist organization first bombed the World Trade Center in New York. Five people were killed and more than 1,000 injured.

Several months prior to this devastating event, the same organization took credit for killing numerous Israeli citizens. Enough was enough! Prime Minister Rabin of Israel took the humane action of temporarily deporting more than 400 Hamas leaders to Lebanon. This was better that the fate of their fellow terrorists in Egypt where the Egyptian authorities killed dozens of them and put hundreds more in prison.

As to be expected, the UN Security Council passed a resolution strongly condemning Israel for ousting these terrorists who are totally committed to the destruction of Israel and the West. The Western media spewed out their pro-Arab propaganda in order to brainwash the American public with their anti-Israel bias which they call "news."

Just when the average American citizen was about to believe that Hamas was a nice group of humanitarians victimized by the oppressive Israelis, they bombed the World Trade Center. What poor timing!

All of a sudden, the American public awakened to the terrorist threat that Israelis face daily. The relatives of those who perished in the 1993 bombing demanded blood. The American congress introduced a bill that would deny members of Hamas visas to enter the country as well as deporting known members of Hamas. How ironic that we have been so quick to condemn the Israelis in their humane treatment of terrorists for over forty years while we want to kill and expel the terrorists after a single incident.

The Hamas organization is not a fringe Islamic sect. Their charter and terrorism represent the mainstream of Islamic fundamentalist thinking that is threatening to overthrow Arab governments, annihilate Israel and humble the West. They have established an extensive support network in the United States to aid its reign of terror around the world.

The attack on the World Trade Center in 1993 was only a dress rehearsal for the horror that would come later. As the whole world knows, on September 11, 2001, radical Islamic fundamentalists hijacked four planes. Two of these planes were flown into the towering, twin World Trade Center buildings, which represented the financial heart of America. Many thousands of innocent people were murdered, and the buildings were completely destroyed.

The terrorists hijacked a third plane and flew it into the Pentagon, the headquarters in Washington, DC, for the American military. Hundreds more were killed. If that was not enough shock for us all, the terrorists hijacked a fourth plane but failed to reach its target. The courageous passengers on the plane forced the plane to crash in the woods of Pennsylvania. Analysts have speculated that the hijackers wanted to crash the plane into the White House.

While Osama bin Laden is blamed for this horrific act of terrorism, there is no difference between any of these terrorist groups. No matter their name, Hamas, Al-Qaeda, Hezbollah, Islamic Jihad, Al-Aksa Brigade, etc., they all have the same goal to destroy Israel and America. And while we should all sympathize for the desperate conditions of the self-proclaimed Palestinian Arabs, we must remember that they elected Hamas as their government. I say self-proclaimed Palestinian Arabs because as you will discover in a later chapter, never in history has there even been a "Palestinian People." By electing Hamas to represent them, they have voted a terrorist group to lead them in their fight against Israel. The only difference between Hamas and the so-called moderate Palestinian Authority courted by the U.S. Statement Department is how to best eliminate Israel.

The American government has declared this attack to be an act of war and has promised to destroy the bases and infrastructures of terrorists wherever they may be found. This is a just but difficult goal as we have discovered in our attempt to capture Osama bin Laden and his Al-Qaeda terrorist group.

While only the Almighty knows the outcome of our war against terrorism, one thing we mortals can know for sure is that the world will never be the same.

ISLAM ON THE MOVE

Islam is clearly on the move. It is no longer the desert religion of the Middle East. Its tentacles have reached around the globe in an effort to achieve world domination through territorial conquest and the complete submission of all people to Allah. The modern revival of Islam, fueled by unrestrained nationalistic fervor, has become the most powerful and dangerous force in our world. Yet, the Western world knows so little about Islam and finds it hard to believe what we do learn.

While there are numerous militant Islamic terrorist groups, they all want to impose their extremist's views on the nations of the world. Since Israel lives in a "tough neighborhood" that is surrounded by states that sponsor and protect these terrorists, Israel has suffered the brunt of their hatred.

For the Islamic fundamentalists, all nations must be converted to Islam. Christians and Jews may, however, retain their faith as "People of the Book" on conditions they submit to

Muslim sovereignty. The notion that Muslims must live under non-Muslim governments, as in Israel or the USA, is totally unacceptable to these people.

Peace-loving Arab Muslims (and Christians) who do not share the hatred against the West, and who refuse to cooperate with the militants, are also threatened. So it is essential for Americans and Christians around the world to understand that while most terrorists are Muslims, not all Arab Muslims are terrorists. Most Arabs are normal people trying to live their lives in peace with their neighbors. This book is not an anti-Arab Muslim book. The One True God loves everyone the same. But He does not love nor does He condone evil.

Some who are hostile to Jews and hostile to Israel try to justify the heinous terrorist attacks in the U.S. by citing American support for Israel. But we must remember, that militant Islamic hatred of America would occur regardless of whether Israel existed or not.

Islamic Hatred of America and Israel

Radical Islamic terrorists hold extreme anti-Semitic and anti-Christian views and wish to see the outbreak of a religious war. They see themselves as the "revengers" for the Crusades, which happened a thousand years ago, and the restorers of Islamic pride.

Furthermore, they despise America and the West because of their deep, abiding resentment of America's religious freedom, political plurality, equality of the sexes, and America's economic superiority. They feel this puts them in an unacceptable position of inferiority, which they seek to change by violence.

This is why Muslim terrorists chant, "Today we fight the Saturday people (Jews), tomorrow the Sunday people (Christians)." The fight against the Saturday people has been going on in Israel for decades. The fight against the Sunday people was revealed to the whole world on September 11, 2001.

The first American led coalition against Iraq, with Christian solders based in Saudi Arabia, was a humiliating defeat and setback for the militant Islamic groups. This inflamed their hatred of the "Christian West" led by America. Since the Gulf War, they have planned and successfully carried out attacks against American interests overseas. The last American led coalition to disarm Iraq has certainly caused more hatred against America.

With years of "sleeper" cells planted in America, militant Islamic terrorists now believe they can demoralize and destroy America from within, thus removing the greatest obstacle to their dream of world conquest. While it will be a long, difficult, and painful struggle against terrorism, the ancient words of the Hebrew prophets give certain hope and comfort for the future for those who have a Judeo-Christian heritage:

> *Now it shall come to pass in the latter days that the mountain of the Lord's house shall be established on the top of the mountains, and shall be exalted above the hills; and all nations shall flow to it. Many shall come and say, "Come, and let us go up to the mountain of the Lord, to the house of the God of Jacob; He will teach us His ways, and we will walk in His paths." For out of Zion shall forth the law, and the word of the Lord from Jerusalem. He shall judge between the nations, and rebuke many people; they shall beat their swords into plowshares, and their spears into pruning hooks; nation shall not lift up sword against nation, neither shall the learn war anymore* (Isaiah 2:2-4).

LOOKING AHEAD

As an author of 30 books, I cannot think of any subject more relevant to our world today than the subject of this book. Because the subject is Islam, the first chapters introduce Islam to the Western, Judeo-Christian reader. The chapters that follow explain Middle East Myths regarding the Arab-Israeli conflict that most American people believe to be true simply because the American media repeats them over and over. I have personally been to Israel over thirty times. I have seen for myself what is happening in Israel. In these chapters I am basically reporting to you what I have learned as if I was there as your representative. In the next chapters, I explain how the God of the Bible is fulfilling biblical prophecy to bring the Jews back to their ancient homeland and the Christian's responsibility to participate in this divine process that will bring redemption to the whole world.

My purpose for writing this book is to enlighten you to this most important subject and to encourage you as you discover that the One True God is a God of love who will in His own way and time cause nations to beat their swords into plowshares and study war no more. Good will triumph over evil, love will triumph over hate. The God of Abraham, Isaac, and Jacob will redeem and restore fallen mankind. Until then, radical Islam is invading us with its anti-Judeo-Christian agenda as discussed in the next chapter. Get ready to read some startling statements by Islamic leaders that should make every Christian and Jew prepare themselves for the Islamic invasion of America and the West.

Chapter 1

The Islamic Invasion of America and the West

In spite of some who want to revise American history, our country was founded by godly Christians fleeing Britain for the purpose of religious freedom. This is not just my opinion. Anyone can learn this by simply reading books by and about the Pilgrims and Puritans who came to America.

Of the many good books available, one of the most interesting is entitled, *Of Plymouth Plantation.* This fascinating book traces the history of the New Plymouth Settlement from its inception on British soil in 1608, to its sojourn in the Netherlands, and finally to its establishment on American shores. It is actually the diary of William Bradford's history of the Plymouth Settlement from 1608-1650. Bradford served as governor of the new colony and faithfully recorded his first-hand account of life at Plymouth.

These founders of our country had a strong connection to the Hebrew Bible (what Christians call the Old Testament). They studied the Hebrew language and knew well the biblical Hebraic-Jewish roots of Christianity. They had a strong Judeo-Christian heritage. They came with a Bible in one hand and faith in the other hand. I am most grateful that our founding fathers brought religious freedom to America. But with all due respect to the first elected Muslim congressman from Minnesota, there was no Koran on the Mayflower. My point is that America was founded on the basis of a Judeo-Christian heritage. Historically Americans were raised with the Bible. Since there is nothing about Islam in the Bible, the American people know little or nothing about the life of Mohammed and the teachings of Islam. That is why in these first chapters I give a brief survey about the growth of Islam, what Islam believes and practices and how this differs from Christian teachings. Let's begin in this chapter with some startling facts about the growth of Islam.

FACTS ABOUT THE GROWTH OF ISLAM

Islam is one of the world's fastest-growing religions, gaining converts in every country through an aggressive missionary program. The worldwide Islamic population has now reached one billion. This means that one in every five persons is now a Muslim.

The majority of the populations of eleven of the twenty-five, fastest-growing nations in the world are Muslim. It is even more frightening to realize that these predominately Muslim populations are growing at a staggering rate. The birthrate in Muslim countries is 42 per 1,000 compared to 13 per 1,000 in the West.[1]

Islam dominates 38 countries in the Middle East, Asia and Africa and is spreading rapidly in the West. For example, in England, the birthplace of John Wesley, there are more Muslims than Methodists. There are thousands of Mosques in England and the number continues to grow. This is also true of every European country.[2]

In the United States, Islam claims to be the fourth largest religion. Muslims are outnumbered only by Southern Baptist, Roman Catholics, and those who practice Judaism. There are more Muslims in the United States than Methodists, Lutherans, Presbyterians, Episcopalians, etc. In the near future, there will be more Muslims than Jews in the United States. Think about that!

You would think that the events of September 11, 2001 would discourage Muslims from coming to America. But just the opposite has happened. According to an article appearing in the Houston Chronicle, September 20, 2006, page A14, more Muslims are immigrating to America than ever before. The article reports that in 2005, 96,000 people from Muslim countries became legal permanent residents of the U.S. This is more than in the previous two decades. Quoting the Department of Homeland Security, the article goes on to say that more than 40,000 immigrants from Muslim countries were admitted to the U.S. in 2006.[3]

America is the greatest country in the world, and I understand why people want to come here. Those who want to come to America to make a better life for themselves should have that opportunity. That is not the point. The point is that the people coming to America do not have a Judeo-Christian heritage. Over time, this pattern of immigration will greatly change America. As one Muslim leader in the U.S. has said, "Most of our urban centers will be predominantly Muslim by 2020."[4]

The number of Mosques being built in America is growing daily. Saudi money finances the building of these Mosques. The problem is not the building of Mosques because America has freedom of religion. The problem is that these Mosques represent the radical Wahhabi brand of Islam practiced by the founders of Saudi Arabia including Osama bin Ladin. If you are a Jew or a Christian, would you want a Mosque in your neighborhood that teaches this form of Islam?

In addition, the Saudis give millions of dollars every year to American Universities to fund Islamic Studies Departments with the stipulation that the universities would hire Islamic professors to chair the department and teach the courses. It makes sense that Islamic professors would teach Islamic studies. Again, that is not the point. The point is that Islamic professors at universities across America are teaching something other than a Judeo-Christian tradition and heritage to their students.

The same is true in our lower level schools where children role-play being a Muslim and are taught Islamic values. Can you imagine these same schools requiring children to role-play being a Christian or a Jew? While it is always good to learn about other cultures and faiths, these children will be brought up with an Islamic world-view, not the Judeo-Christian tradition that made America great.

Furthermore, Saudi money helps finance the political campaigns of many of our public officials as well as those who have retired from government. For example, one only has to look at the source of much of the funding for former President Carter's Research Center in Atlanta or the Baker Institute for Public Policy in Houston to understand why these organizations are anti-Semitic. Just follow the money trail and it leads to Saudi Arabia. Those with money have a tendency to give for the purpose of influencing those who are the beneficiaries of that money. This is human nature which we all understand. Again, this is not the point. The point is that these politicians and political organizations are influenced to promote pro-Saudi agendas that are opposed to our Judeo-Christian heritage.

America is a nation of immigrants. Honorable people who want to come to America to make a better life for themselves and who are willing to live according to our way of life, certainly should be given the opportunity. But in the name of freedom and political correctness, our government leaders have opened our society at the highest levels to terrorists who present themselves as good, loyal American Muslims.

Our founding fathers were clear in their beliefs that our form of government would only work with moral citizens who make decisions based on Judeo-Christian values. We are a self-governing people. As our nation removes these values from public life, our beloved America will continue to crumble. The agenda of radical Islam is to hasten the day when America will not have the moral clarity and strength to stand against their onslaught on our culture. Our democracy will give way to anarchy unless the American people return to our Judeo-Christian heritage.

THE ISLAMIZATION OF AMERICA

It is the goal of radical Islam to destroy our Judeo-Christian culture, heritage and Constitution and replace it with Islam and Islamic law with an American Muslim as President of the United States. In his book, *The Islamization of America*, Abdullah Al-Araby, gives the following comments by Muslim leaders expressing their true goal regarding the transformation of America from a Judeo-Christian nation to an Islamic nation.

He reports that during an official meeting on Islamic-Christian dialogue, the Muslim leader explained to the Christians participating, "Thanks to your democratic laws we will invade you; thanks to our religious laws we will dominate you."[5]

As far back as 1983, an influential Muslim leader named Isma'il Al-Farfuqi said, "Nothing could be greater than this youthful, vigorous, and rich continent (North America) turning away from its past evil and marching forward under the banner of Allahu Akbar (Allah is great)."[6]

At the dedication of an Islamic Center on Stockholm, Sweden in 1983, the speaker proclaimed, "In the next 50 years, we will capture the Western world for Islam. We have the men to do it, we have the money to do it, and above all, we are already doing it."[7]

In 1984, the vice president of the Islamic College in Chicago stated, "My dream is that the USA will become an Islamic nation by the year 2000."[8]

Omar Abdel Rahman is the blind sheikh convicted of the attack against the World Trade Center in 1993. In 1991 he called on Muslims to "conquer the lands of the infidels."[9]

Imam Siraj Wahhaj was the first Muslim clergy to offer a prayer in the U.S. House of Representatives. He said, "Take my word, if 6-8 million Muslims unite in America, the country will come to us." He further said, "In time, this so-called democracy will crumble, and there will be nothing. And the only thing that will remain will be Islam."[10]

Imam Zaid Shakir was the former Muslim chaplain at Yale University. He indicated that Muslims cannot accept the legitimacy of the existing (American) system."[11]

Another Muslim leader, Adman Nawfal, has said, "It will be very easy for us to preside over this world once again."[12]

One month after September 11, 2001, a Muslim speaker at a convention in San Jose declared, "By the year 2020, we should have an American-Muslim President of the United States."[13]

Abdurahman M. Alamoudi is the influential founder of the American Muslim Council. He has told his Muslim audiences that the goal of Muslims in America is to turn the U.S. into an Islamic state, even if it takes "a hundred years." He further says, "If we are outside the country [America], we can say, "O Allah, destroy America. But once we are here, our mission in this country is to change it."[14]

Alamoudi was put in jail after pleading guilty to plotting acts of terrorism. Before then, he was an advisor to the Pentagon on Islam. In this capacity he created the Muslim chaplain corps in the U.S. military and placed Muslim chaplains in the military.

Omar M. Ahmad is the chairman of the Council of American-Islamic Relations better known as CAIR. CAIR is the "Islamic organization" of choice in Washington. It has tremendous favor and influence. While claiming to be an organization of peace and tolerance, CAIR recently barred the Christian Broadcasting Network from attending a CAIR press conference. Ahmad says, "Islam isn't in America to be equal to any other faith, but to dominate. The Koran should be the highest authority in America."[15]

In his startling book, *Inflitration*, investigative journalist Paul Sperry, provides shocking facts about the radical Muslim agenda to destroy our way of life. He quotes Donald Lavey who is an FBI counterterrorism veteran who also served as counterterrorism chief for Interpol:

> Muslim subversives have managed to build an impressing infrastructure of support for the bad guys like al-Qaida terrorist. Muslim subversives have been working clandestinely to undermine America's constitutional government and the Judeo-Christianity on which it was built. Their goal is to replace the U.S. Constitution with the Koran and turn America into an Islamic state. Their strategy is to exploit the very rights and freedoms they intend to banish, while counting on the ever-trusting American people to remain blind to their true intentions.[16]

Sperry says that radical Islamists have infiltrated every level of American life and cites the following alarming examples.[17]

1. A senior White House official of Persian origin has been put in charge of government contracting and

outsourcing, even though congressional lobbying records show he once lobbied on behalf of a Muslim activist who is now a confessed terrorist.

2. The same official prior to 9/11 lobbied Congress and federal agencies to make it harder for federal law enforcement to deport Middle Eastern immigrants with suspected terror links.
3. An Islamic activist obtained a sensitive intelligence post at the Department of Homeland Security even though he failed to disclose his past association with the same confessed terrorist.
4. In their rush to recruit Arabic translators after 9/11, both the FBI and the Pentagon cut corners on background checks and hired Muslim translators in spite of their ties to various foreign military and intelligence agencies in Syria, Egypt, Pakistan, and Turkey. Of course the translators can tell the FBI anything they want and the FBI would not be the wiser. At the same time, none of the 60 Arab-speaking Jews who applied were accepted because the Muslims would not work with them.
5. Laptops with classified intelligence about al-Qaida investigations have gone missing from the translation unit in the Washington field office of the FBI.
6. The FBI hired the daughter of a former senior Pakistani intelligent officer to translate the intercepts of Pakistani targets. About 6 months later, a secret FBI code was compromised, falling into the hands of the Pakistani government.
7. A Muslim FBI agent refused to wear a wire to secretly record a Muslim target of counterterrorism

investigation because he was a friend of the person being investigated.

8. A Palestinian activist, who sponsors an orphaned child of a Palestinian suicide bomber, has free access to the White House through Karl Rove, the President's friend and political advisor.

9. President Bush struck a deal with Muslim-rights groups to avoid describing terrorism as "Islamic."

10. CAIR (the Council of American-Islamic Relations) is considered one of the most respectable and influential mainstream Islamic organizations in America with an open door to Washington's elite. Yet, it has donated money to known terrorist organizations and three of its former top officials have been arrested for terrorist-related activities.

11. CAIR receives large sums of money from Islamic groups in the Middle-East with ties to terrorists.

12. CAIR has successfully won more than two hundred cases against U.S. companies for alleged discrimination against Muslims.

14. A Muslim social studies teacher who was on the Saudi government payroll is educating your children about Islam in public schools through sugar-coated textbooks and role-playing exercises in which kids "pretend to be Muslims" for weeks. Furthermore, the Saudi's are giving millions of dollars to schools to fund their pro-Muslim propaganda through textbooks, teachers, and professors and establishing pro-Islamic Studies Department in major universities.

15. Saudi Arabia is also financing, with money from Islamic radicals, thousands of synagogues around the country with an Islamic fundamentalist message.

16. A large influential Mosque in Washington DC was the "home synagogue" of two of the Saudi hijackers who attacked the Pentagon buildings. The Mosque is owned and controlled by Saudi Islamic fundamentalists. At least four of the leaders of the Mosque have now been investigated for terrorist ties.

17. There are an estimated 200,000 Muslim inmates in our prison system. Most are African-American converts, and many are eligible for parole. Their Islamic chaplains are preparing them for their new life of freedom as radical Muslims who hate white people and the white people's Judeo-Christian racist religion that enslaves them.

18. According to a leasing agent and former residents, the Saudi diplomats who stay at a Pentagon-area apartment building cheered the 9/11 attacks.

19. Finally, U.S. intelligence tells us that al-Qaida has trained approximately 120,000 terrorist. Thanks to our "open door policies" for immigrants and people who sneak across our borders, it is estimated that we have about 5,000 of these terrorists in the U.S.

In his excellent booklet, *The Shadow of the Crescent*, Robert Peck explains that the first great influx of Muslims to the U.S. happened during the times of African slave trade to America. The next major immigration of Muslims to the U.S. came in the 1860s when large numbers of Muslims fled Syria and Lebanon to avoid military service in the Turkish army. In the 1940s another wave of immigrants came to the shores of the U.S. to escape the civil war between Pakistan and India. Further immigration to the

U.S. came later when Moslems were fleeing political and economic troubles in Turkey.[18]

According to Peck, most of the Muslims who were early migrants to the U.S. were only marginally observant. They were cultural Muslims who could embrace our nation's ideas and values. However, in the last thirty years, Muslim immigrants to the U.S. are much more observant and idealistic in their beliefs and practices. They have a religious, evangelistic fervor to establish Islamic influence in America.[19]

Peck explains that the Muslim population and influence in America is growing because of an increase in immigration, a high birth rate among Muslims, intermarriage of Muslim men with non-Muslim American women and conversion.[20]

In his outstanding book, *America Alone*, Mark Steyn, reports the frightening birthrate statistics of European countries compared to Islamic nations. He says that for a nation to sustain itself, it must have a fertility rate of 2.1 live births per woman.[21] He points out that any country that drops below this rate for an extended period of time will not survive.[22] He then gives the following alarming birth statistics: America, 2.1; Canada, 1.48; Japan, 1.32; Russia, 1.14; Greece, 1,3; Spain 1.1; Italy, 1.2, and Europe as a whole 1.38.[23] From these statistics, America is the only country "holding its own."

Mark Steyn goes on to observe that "much of what we loosely call the Western world will not survive the twenty-first century, and much of it will effectively disappear within our lifetimes, including many if not most European countries."[24] Mark believes that Europe will be semi-Islamic in its politico-cultural character within a generation.[25]

It doesn't take a statistician to understand the significance of these facts. Christians and Jews must learn as much as possible about Islam and stand together against radical Islamic terrorists who want to destroy our way of life. Europe, including Britain, is already referred to as Eurabia. It is a post-Christian Europe. Unless there is a last minute cultural and spiritual awakening, Europe will fall internally to Islam.

Ron Peck asks the question, "Will the crescent replace the Cross in America?"[26] Will America go the way of Europe? Will Christians and Jews in America awaken to this threat before it is too late or remain ignorant and indifferent? We live the good live in America. Why should we even care? I think the answer will be obvious when you understand the basic teachings and practices of Islam and its controversial founder discussed in the next chapters.

The information presented in this chapter should certainly awaken Christians and Jews to the radical Islam threat to America and our way of life. Only God knows if the American government and people will have the moral clarity and will to stand against this invasion. But one thing we can know for sure, the One True God of heaven does have the moral clarity and will to establish His kingdom on the earth. When all is said and done, the God of Abraham, Isaac and Jacob will execute judgment on His enemies. He will rule over the nations and His people with a righteous government that will bring peace to the earth.

Personal Study Review

1. What are your thoughts about the statement, "There was no Koran on the Mayflower"?
2. Why do you think Europe is becoming Islamic?
3. Why do you think America is vulnerable to the "Islamic invasion?"
4. How should Jews and Christians respond to this invasion?

Chapter 2

ISLAM: BELIEFS AND PRACTICES

The word *Islam* is an Arabic word which means "submission or surrender." Within the context of Islam, it means submission or surrender to Allah, the god of Islam. A follower of Islam is called a *Muslim* or *Moslem*, which simply means "one who submits." The purpose of this chapter is to introduce the basic teachings and practices of this religion that radical Islamists want the world to submit to and which they seek to enforce by violent means.

THE FIVE DOCTRINES OF ISLAM

Islam teaches five basic doctrines or beliefs which are summarized below. These teachings of Islam will be further discussed and compared to Christian teachings in Chapter 4.

1. *God*

   Islam is a monotheistic religion in that it teaches belief in one god. In Islam, there is only one true god and his name is Allah. Allah is all-seeing, all-knowing, and all-powerful. This is the most important declaration of the Moslem faith. As we study Islam's view of Allah, we discover that Allah is an impersonal deity who cannot be known and loved. He can only be feared and obeyed. Allah is absolute in his power and his will is supreme but his character is not one of love and grace.[1] I wish I could say different, but Allah is not a heavenly Father waiting to embrace and comfort his children with arms of love.

The world believes that Jews, Christians, and Muslims worship the same God but by a different name. However, as we will discover in later chapters, there are many differences between the Yahweh of the Bible and the Allah of the Koran. As we will learn, the Koran itself makes a distinction between the Judeo-Christian God and Allah.

2. *Prophets*

The Koran mentions 28 prophets of Allah. The six greatest are: Adam, Noah, Abraham, Moses, Jesus, and Mohammed. According to the Koran, Mohammed is the last and greatest of these prophets. He is considered the "Seal of the Prophets," after whom there can be no more. Islam considers all prophets in the Bible as being Islamic predecessors to Mohammed. In other words, Islam teaches that Adam, Noah, Abraham, Moses and Jesus were Muslims who worshiped Allah. This means that Muslims consider Islam to be the first and oldest monotheistic religion in the world. Since Mohammed is the last and greatest prophet, Islam teaches that he clarified the teachings of previous prophets by putting their words within the context of Islam.[2]

3. ***Scripture***

According to Islam, there are four God-inspired books. These are: 1) the Torah of Moses, 2) the Psalms of David, 3) the Gospel of Jesus, and 4) the Koran. While Islam recognizes the writings of the Hebrew Bible and the New Testament, it claims that the words in the Bible were corrupted by Jews and Christians and are not valid revelations. Therefore, they are untrustworthy and are not the true word of God. This means there is no basis for discussing the Bible with Muslims since they believe it is corrupted. While this is what Islam teaches about the Bible, they cannot point to any time or event in history when this corruption of the Bible supposedly happened. The bottom line is that Islam teaches that the Koran is Allah's final word to mankind which supersedes all previous, sacred writings.[3]

In addition to the Koran, Islam reveres two additional texts—the Hadith (Tradition) and the Sunnah. The Hadith is a collection of sayings and commandments attributed to Mohammed while the Sunnah is the basis of Islamic legal code called *shari'a*, meaning "the path." It is the authoritative rule book governing Islamic life. It includes events in the life of Mohammed and gives examples for Muslims to follow in their practice of Islam.[4] The most accepted version of the Hadith is that compiled by Sahih Al-Bukhari.[5]

The Hadith and Sunnah relate to the Koran much like the Talmud and Mishna relate to the Tanakh (Hebrew Bible) in that they help explain the life of Mohammed, his teachings and ways to practice what is written in the Koran. It is in these books that we read what we would consider to be most bizarre statements attributed to Mohammed. According to the Hadith, Mohammed made the following statements: [6]

- Drinking camel urine will make you healthy (7.590).
- Fever comes from the heat of hell (7.619).
- A fly in your drink can cure you of disease (4.537).
- If you speak badly about a deceased person, that person will go to hell (2.448).
- Women are deficient in mind (2.541; 3.826).
- The majority of people in hell are women (1.28; 3.01; 2.161; 7.124).
- Women are a bad omen (7.30).
- The sex of a child is determined by whether the man or the woman had the first orgasm (5.275).

4. *Angels*

Since Mohammed claimed that his revelations came from the angel Gabriel, a belief in angels is essential to the Muslim faith. Islam teaches that there are good angels and fallen angels. Gabriel is the chief, good angel, while Shaytan (Satan) is the ruler of the fallen angels, which are called Jinn (demons).

Dr. Anis Shorrosh, in his book, *Islam Revealed*, explains, "Muslims believe in four archangels: Gabriel (the angel of revelation), Michael (the angel of providence), Israfil (the angel of doom), and Izra'il (the angel of death). Ministering angels include recording angels, throne-bearers, and questioners of the dead. A third category is the fallen angels, the chief of which is Iblis, or Shaytan. A fourth group includes Jinn genii, a group of spirits midway between men and angels, some good and some bad." [7]

5. ***Judgment***

According to Islam, the last day will be a time of resurrection and judgment. Allah will be the judge and each person will be sent to heaven (a place of sensual pleasure) or hell (a terrible place of torment) on the basis of their acceptance of Allah. Tragically for Muslims, they never know if Allah will accept them or not. Even Mohammed did not know his fate. He said, "By Allah, though I am the Apostle of Allah, yet I do not know what Allah will do to me" (Hadith 5.266).

Since Muslims do not know their fate, they must be promised some kind of reward for their obedience to Allah. And what greater reward than sensual pleasures that would appeal to a seventh century Arab male. As Dr. Anis Shorrosh explains, "Pious believers in Allah can expect abundant sensual pleasures in Paradise. There will be perpetual luxury, physical comfort, food, clean water, mansions, servants, lovely maidens, and virgins." [8]

This is why Islamic leaders promise that a Paradise with 72 virgins awaits devout Muslims who commit terrorist acts of suicide killing infidels (Jews and Christians) for the cause of Allah. I cannot image the One True God hating anything more than this despicable lie. As a Western person, it is hard to grasp how modern people can be so brainwashed and deceived to believe such things. Unfortunately, the truth is many Arab people still live with a seventh century mindset.

THE FIVE PILLARS OF THE FAITH

In addition to these five basic doctrines, Islam teaches that there are five "pillars" of the faith. These are the primary religious duties or practices of Muslims. The five are summarized as follows.

1. ***Statement of Belief***

   Muslims believe that there is no God but Allah, and Mohammed is the prophet of Allah. They are required to confess this belief aloud, in public, several times a day and proclaim his greatness (Allah Akhbar) when murdering others in his name. This statement of belief is the core creed of Islam. By confessing this creed, Muslims proclaim their strict allegiance to Allah and his messenger.[9]

   Muslims repeat this confession in a way similar to the Jewish people reciting the *Shema* from Deuteronomy 6:4, "Here, O Israel; The Lord our God, the Lord is one." However, as we will see even more clearly, the Muslims are confessing a different god than that of the Jews. Also, by acknowledging Mohammed, they are following a different prophet than the Jews who acknowledge Moses.

2. ***Prayers***

   Muslims are required to pray five times a day while facing Mecca. These prescribed prayers must be said upon rising, at noon, in mid-afternoon, after sunset and before retiring.[10]

   When Mohammed went to Medina, he told the Jews that Allah instructed him to pray facing Jerusalem. But when the Jews rejected Mohammed, he received a new revelation from Allah to pray facing Mecca.[11]

Today, devout Muslims pray facing Mecca (not Jerusalem). As just mentioned, these are not personal prayers from the heart but prescribed prayers that the faithful have memorized. They do not connect the worshipers in a personal intimate way with Allah.

The haunting call to prayer is sounded at the appropriate time of day from the mosque. The one who calls the worshipers to prayer is called a "muezzin." He does this from a high tower in the mosque which is called a "minaret."You hear this call to prayer throughout the day in the Middle East.

3. *Almsgiving*

Islam requires Muslims to give 2.5 per cent of their income to the poor and to the Mosque. While this is considerably less than the tithe (10 per cent) mentioned in the Bible, it is a duty expected of all Muslims. Charity and almsgiving is certainly a good practice. Whereas almsgiving in the Judeo-Christian tradition is a matter of the heart, in Islam it is a duty by which the worshiper hopes to earn the mercy of Allah.[12]

4. *Fasting*

Muslims are required to fast during the daylight hours of the Islamic holy month of Ramadan. During this time of fasting, Muslims may not consume food or drink between sunrise and sunset. Caner comments that fasting is an annual, lifelong requirement for every devout Muslim.[13] He adds, "The Muslim, from sunrise to sunset, is required to abstain from sexual intercourse, eating, drinking, and smoking. In its place, he is to read the Koran introspectively, performing an act of worship in his or her self-restraint."[14]

5. *The Hajj - Pilgrimage to Mecca*

   Every Muslim is required to make at least one pilgrimage to Mecca in his lifetime.[15] A Muslim who is physically unable to make the pilgrimage because of poor health or advanced age may send another in his place. Mecca, not Jerusalem, is the Islamic "holy city." Jerusalem is important to the Arab people from a political viewpoint, not a spiritual one.

   The main focus at the shrine at Mecca is the "Kaaba." The Kaaba is a stone building some thirty-three feet wide, forty feet long, and fifty feet high. It houses a black stone, thought to be a meteorite, where Islam teaches that Abraham offered Ishmael as a sacrifice. Since God offered a ram in place of Ishmael, Islam teaches that Abraham built the Kaaba in gratitude as a place to worship Allah and requested that people make an annual pilgrimage there in honor of the event.[16]

   Referring to the George Braswell book, *What you Need to Know About Islam and Muslims*,(Broadman and Holman), Caner and Caner give the following description of the pilgrimage. "Only Muslims are allowed inside the city of Mecca, and all are required to dress in a simple white robe. The pilgrims first cleanse themselves before they begin their ritual. The first stage begins as thousands circle the Kaaba seven times, reciting verses from the Koran and offering prayers along the way.

   "The circling of the Kaaba, however, is just the beginning of the journey. Muslims also must run seven times between the two hills of Mecca, reenacting Hagar's frantic search for water for her son Ishmael. Finally, pilgrims find water at the well of Zamzam and take a drink, displaying the fulfillment of Hagar's quest for her son's needs.

"Now immersed in the journey, the pilgrims must yet travel a long way in order to accomplish their duty.

- They must travel 13 miles to the plain of Arafat, where Mohammed preached his last sermon.
- Here, they stand from noon to sunset in honor of Mohammed's exalted position in the community.
- Pilgrims must go to Mina, the site of the sacrifice of Ishmael by his father Abraham. Here pilgrims throw seven stones, memorializing how Ishmael threw stones at the Devil to resist temptations.
- Next, pilgrims sacrifice an animal in remembrance of the ram offered in place of Ishmael.
- Muslims return to Mecca and repeat their encircling of the Kaaba and running of the hills.[17]
- As we will discover in the next chapter, these are the same rituals performed by Arabs in their pre-Islamic worship of the Moon god. Mohammed was smart enough to allow the followers of his new religion to continue these practices so they would not have to change their old ways.

Holy War

A sixth unofficial practice concerns the "Jihad" or holy war. The whole world is now familiar with this violent element of Islam. When called upon, Muslim men are obligated to fight in a holy war or Jihad in order to the spread Islam or defend Islam against the infidels (Jews and Christians), or any other religion. One who dies in a Jihad is guaranteed a place in heaven where seventy-two virgins are waiting to beckon to their every need.[18]

In spite of the reassuring words of our politically correct leaders, the truth is Islam has a bloody history. Unfortunately, this is the norm, not an exception as in the days of the "Christian Crusades." This history is clearly documented and readily available to anyone willing to take the time to discover it. It grieves me to say that Christianity also has a bloody history but not as a part of Christian theology. Historically, Islam expanded through military conquest. Radical Islamists react to every criticism with violence. They deny it is violent by committing acts of violence. We see this manifested every day around the world where Islamic fundamentalist kill as many people as they can in their misguided zeal.

The Ayatollah Khomeini said, "The purest joy in Islam is to kill and be killed for Allah."[19] Islamic terrorists truly believe that killing the infidels (Jews and Christians) draws them closer to Allah. Every week Islamic spiritual leaders exhort the faithful to practice Jihad in the name of Allah.

I wish I could say that the horrific events of 9/11 were the results of a few misguided Islamic fanatics. But unfortunately, this is not true. Islam uses the sword as the key to Paradise. No matter how many times we are reassured that Islam is a peaceful religion, their leaders commit more atrocities in the name of their god. We will read the words of Jihad in a later chapter and see clearly the violent nature of Islam.

ISLAMIC SECTS

When Mohammed died, he had not appointed a successor. He was succeeded by four rulers who fought over control of the new faith. These were Abu Bakr (632-634), Umar (634-644), Uthman (644-656), and Ali (656-661). The fourth successor, or Caliph, Ali Abu Talib, was Mohammed's cousin. In addition, Ali was married to Mohammed's only daughter, Fatima.

Three of the Caliph's (Mohammed's successors), including Ali and two of his sons, were murdered while battling factional rivals for leadership of the growing Islamic empire. Ali's second son was named Hussein. When he and his family were killed, the animosity between the two factions intensified. These power struggles caused a major split in the Islamic world which continues to this day.[20]

While there are many Islamic sects, the two primary ones caused by the early split are the Sunni Muslims and the Shiite (Shia) Muslims. Sunni Muslims are the largest in the Muslim world. They acknowledge the first four Caliphs as the true successors of Mohammed. Their name comes from the Arabic word *sunnah*, meaning "tradition." They were primarily based in Mecca and wanted to choose a successor to Mohammed based on tribal loyalties and traditions. They preferred the traditions of their elders in determining who would succeed Mohammed as their spiritual leader.

Over time, the Sunni Muslims developed the Islamic rule of law (sharia) to govern the faithful. It is based on the Koran, the Hadith and the interpretations of Islamic scholars. About eight-five percent of the one billion Muslims is Sunni.[21] Historically; the Sunni have been the more moderate of the two sects.

The Shiite (followers or faction of Ali) was centered in Medina, about two hundred miles north of Mecca. They rejected the rule by the Caliphs and maintained that only Mohammed's direct blood line descendants beginning with Ali could succeed him. They replaced the Caliphs with their own spiritual leaders called, *imams*.[22] Historically, the Shiites have represented the radical fringe of Islam. Shiite Muslims are the minority sect, but they make up 95 percent of the population of Iran and Iraq.

When America toppled Saddam Hussein, a non-observant Sunni, the Shiite majority in Iraq saw this as their opportunity to take revenge against the ruling Sunni Muslims. This is what they are fighting about among themselves in Iraq. This is also why Iran is supporting their Shiite brothers in Iraq. Unfortunately, the American military is caught in the cross fires of this conflict between the Sunni and the Shiite factions.

In the Shiite tradition, the *imam* is a Charismatic spiritual leader who faithfully interprets Islamic law and tradition with the spiritual anointing and authority of Mohammed. Shiites believe that the *imam* is a direct descendant of Ali and that there were twelve of these direct descendants. They believe that the twelfth descendant never died but that Allah hid him on the earth until he would be revealed at the end of time.[23] Shiite Muslims believe he will appear on the scene at the end of the age as the "Mahdi," or "expected one" similar to the Judeo/Christian understanding of the coming Messiah.

The President of Iran, Mahmoud Ahmadinejad, is a devout believer in the soon appearance of the Mahdi. In fact, he believes it is his duty to prepare the way for his appearance.

The Iranian President gave a speech on November 16, 2005 in which he said that his main mission is to "prepare the path for the glorious reappearance of Imam Mahdi, may Allah hasten his appearance." He also claimed that during a speech he gave to the United Nations in the fall of 2005 that he was suddenly surrounded by a supernatural aura when he mentioned the name of Mohammed. He claimed it was a light from heaven confirming his prophetic destiny. He claims that those listening were so enraptured with his speech that they were not able to even blink their eyes. This is a mad man wanting nuclear weapons.

According to the Shiite understanding of the end times, the nations will be at war when the Mahdi returns to bring peace and conquer the nations for Allah. Mahmoud Ahmadinejad believes it is his calling in life to initiate war in order to hasten the appearance of the Mahdi. This is why he is pressing forward with his efforts to make Iran a nuclear power, destroy Israel and fight the West.

The Sunnis and Shiites have been bitter enemies for centuries. They constantly war among themselves for control of the Islamic world. We see this power struggle between the Sunni and Shiites played out everyday in Iraq. Ironically, as I was writing this paragraph, a Sunni suicide bomber blew himself up in Iraq killing thirty Shiites and wounding many more. The Shiites were making a pilgrimage to the city of Karbala to pay homage to Hussein. Sunni terrorists have murdered approximately 175 Shiites over a two-day period. While only the Almighty knows the outcome of this internal struggle, we know for sure that they will continue to fight among themselves for the heart and soul of the Muslim people.

The Wahhabis (Radical Sunnis of Arabia)

Perhaps the most aggressive and militant Islamic sect is the Wahhabis. The fanatical Wahabbi sect was founded by Mohammad Ibn Abd al-Wahhab (1703-1791) in Saudi Arabia. He believed that other Islamic sects needed to be purified from what he considered to be unacceptable Islamic practices.[24]

Ibn Abd al-Wahhab was an uncompromising fanatical zealot who considered all who disagreed with him to be heretics and apostates from the true faith. He felt justified to impose his beliefs by force and exercise his authority and rule over neighboring tribes. He did this by declaring holy war (jihad) against his Arab neighbors who would not submit to his views.[25]

Ibn Abd al-Wahhab converted the Saud tribe to his brand of Islam. The chief warlord of the Saud tribe was Abd al-Aziz ibn Saud. Ibn Saud (1880-1953) united the warring tribes of Arabia. After consolidating his power, he established the Kingdom of

Saudi Arabia (1932) and declared Wahhabism as the religion of Saudi Arabia.[26]

The discovery of oil in Saudi Arabia brought untold riches to Ibn Saud and his extended royal family through whom he still rules Saudi Arabia. Working in partnership with the Wahhabi religious leaders, Saudi Arabia has used oil revenues to indoctrinate the Saudi population in Wahhabi views while spending huge sums of money to export Wahhabism throughout the world, including the United States. This includes finances to print and distribute Wahhabi literature, build Wahhabi Mosques, finance terrorism, etc.

The radical Islamic fundamentalist terrorist groups such as Osama bin Laden and those who attacked America on September 11 are Saudi Wahhabis. Their goal is to promote their brand of radical, militant Islam throughout the world, and they will use whatever means necessary. They consider it their sacred duty to establish Islamic Wahhabian rule over all the nations. In their mind, the end justifies the means. The greatest danger from bin Laudin is that he has been able to unite the more traditionally moderate Sunni Muslim majority with the extreme radical Shiite minority.

Saudi political rulers are Wahhabis who must appease their religious leaders but who also depend on the West, particularly America, for oil revenues. At the same time, America, which has a Judeo/Christian history and culture, depends on Saudi oil to support the American economy and way of life. While many blame the American support for Israel for the terrorist attacks on America, the real reason is the ideological, religious, and cultural differences between Judeo/Christianity and Islam.

It is obvious that the beliefs and practices of Islam are different than those presented in the Bible which has guided Western civilization. While people have a free will to believe what they want, they do not have the right to force their beliefs on others.

In the challenging days ahead, the God of Abraham, Isaac, and Jacob will reveal Himself to the world as the One True God. The writer of Psalms gives the following word of assurance, "All the ends of the world shall remember and turn to the Lord. And all the families of the nations shall worship before You. For the kingdom is the Lord's, and He rules over the nations."[27]

Personal Study Review

1. Explain the five doctrines or beliefs of Islam.
2. Explain the five primary religious duties of Muslims.
3. What is the difference between Sunni and Shiite Muslims?
4. Who are the Wahhabis?

Chapter 3

The Life of Mohammed

So far we have learned about the religious and cultural clash between Islam, Judeo-Christianity and the Western world. We learned how Islam is spreading, the five doctrines of Islam, the five pillars of the faith, and the major Islamic sects including the fanatical Wahhabi sect which rules Saudi Arabia and is financing most of the Islamic terrorist activities. In this chapter, we will learn about Mohammed, the desert warrior and prophet who claimed to receive revelations from the angel Gabriel which led to his founding of Islam.

But first, let's discover pre-Islamic worship before the time of Mohammed. You may be surprised to discover that Mohammed sanctified many pre-Islamic worship practices that became a part of Islam. He simply devoted them to one of the existing Arab gods of his time. The world has come to know this pre-Islamic god as Allah.

PRE-ISLAMIC WORSHIP

Islam teaches that Allah is the same as the God of the Bible so that Jews, Christians, and Moslems all worship the same God but by a different name. Furthermore, Islam teaches that it is the successor religion to Judaism and Christianity as part of God's unfolding revelation of truth.

If it is true, as Islam claims, that there is divine continuity from Judaism to Christianity to Islam, and that Islam has replaced Judaism and Christianity as the final true revelation from the Almighty, then Jews and Christians should convert to Islam. This is clearly not my view. To examine these claims, it is important to study pre-Islamic worship before the time of Mohammed.

In ancient pagan times, people worshipped many deities. Most of these were somehow related to nature such as worship of the sun and moon, spirits believed to control the forces of nature such as hurricanes and storms, earthquakes, the seas, the rain, etc. These nature-gods were both masculine and feminine and had different names depending on the country in which they were worshipped.

One of the most common early deities worshipped by pagans was the moon. Dr. Robert Morey, an internationally recognized scholar in the fields of theology and apologetics, has done extensive research of archeological discoveries relating to the ancient worship of the moon. He has written some of his findings in his booklet entitled, *The Moon-god Allah in the Archeology of the Middle East* (The Research and Education Foundation, Newport, PA).

Morey's booklet, other scholarly references, and articles available on the internet, are the sources of the following information which can readily be found in documents on ancient pagan worship. In other words, this is not secret information that can only be found in dusty old books in ancient libraries. Anyone who wants to discover this for him or herself can easily do so with just a minimum effort. It is all well documented.

Those who worshiped the moon as deity believed that the moon god was married to the sun goddess. The stars were their daughters.[1] While we scoff at such beliefs today, it should not be difficult for us to imagine how ancient primitive people could have such ideas.

Archeologists have found many temples to the moon god throughout the Middle East. Based on the vast number of discoveries, it is clear that worship of the moon god was certainly one of the most popular religions of the ancient world.[2]

One of the most important and advanced of the early civilizations was the Sumerians. The Sumerians lived in the area of southern Iraq/Kuwait around 2500 B.C. They were a highly developed people who established organized city-states, gave us the first known form of writing, invented the wheel, and excelled in their study of astrology, science, mathematics, agriculture, law, etc.

When the American forces invaded Baghdad, the citizens looted priceless Sumerian artifacts from the Baghdad museum. Furthermore, Iraq's citizens, known as the Madan, who live where the Tigris and Euphrates meet, believe they are descendants of the ancient Sumerians.

The Sumerians believed in many gods and built temples to them in the form of ziggurats (pyramid-temples that soared to the heavens) as mentioned in Genesis 11. Each ziggurat was dedicated to a specific god whom the Sumerians believed ruled over their city.

The chief god in the city of Ur was the moon god.[3] Bible students recognize Ur as the city where Abraham lived (Genesis 11:31). Haran (Genesis 11:26-32) was also devoted to the moon god.

The Sumerian names for the moon god were Nanna, Suen, and Asimbabbar.[4] Later people groups such as the Assyrians and Babylonians transformed the name Suen into the word sin. This became the name by which the moon god was known.[5]

Like the Christian cross and the Jewish Star of David, those who worshipped the moon god also had a symbol. The symbol of moon god worship was the crescent moon.[6] Ancient pagan people believed that the moon god was married to the sun goddess and the stars were their daughters. Sometime the symbol had three stars representing the three daughters of the moon god.[7]

Throughout the entire Middle East, archeologists have discovered the crescent moon symbol on many different items such as pottery, clay tablets, jewelry, seals, idols, ruins, walls, rocks, etc. Even in Hazor, in northern Israel, a temple dedicated to the moon god was discovered.[8]

In Arabia, archeologists have discovered temples to the moon god, symbols of the crescent moon with the name Sin, and thousands of inscriptions indicating that the dominant religion of pre-Islamic Arabia was the moon god.[9] The archeological evidence is overwhelming proof that moon-god worship was the central worship in pre-Islamic Arabia. One may not like to acknowledge that Islam has its roots in worship of the moon god, but the actual evidence of history is irrefutable.

The Arabian name for the moon god was *al* (the) and *ilah* (God), or *Allah*, which simply means "the god, or the supreme god." He was also known as Hubal, the moon god of Babylon. Allah had no name but attributes that described him. The daughters of the moon god were called, Al-Lat, Al-Uzza, and Manat. Their names are mentioned in the Koran in Surah 53:19-20.[10] The crescent moon of Islam is a representative of the moon god while the star represents his daughters.

Allah was the chief or high god among the gods. A shrine to Allah was built in Mecca. This shrine, the Kaaba, housed 360 gods and a sacred black stone. There are various traditions regarding the origin of the black stone. One tradition discussed in the previous chapter is that the angel Gabriel gave the stone to Abraham to commemorate the site where Abraham supposedly offered Ishmael as a sacrifice.

Another tradition is that the stone fell from the moon and was to be worshipped as a manifestation of the moon god. Moon worshipers bowed in prayer toward Mecca several times a day. As a matter of religious duty, they were expected to make a pilgrimage to Mecca and walk around the stone seven times and kiss it as an act of worship.

Worshipers threw stones at the devil, offered sacrifices to the moon-god, gave alms to the poor in his honor, and fasted during the month of the crescent moon. They put the symbol of the crescent moon on their clothing and houses to show their devotion to the moon god. This was the religion of the Arab people when Mohammed was born.[11]

Sound familiar? Mohammed would sanctify these pagan practices and the Arab way of life which gloried in desert warfare, slavery, polygamy, male dominance of women, etc. Mohammed, allowed his followers to continue these practices in the name of Allah.

Mohammed's Early Life

The following information on the life of Mohammed is readily available for anyone wanting to study on their own. I have tried to present a concise summary that highlights his life without getting the reader bogged down in too much detail.

Mohammed was born in Mecca in the year of A.D. 570. He was born into the Quraish tribe, which at that time ruled the city and surrounding area. As the ruling tribe, they were the guardians of the Kaaba.[12] This means they were the leading family in the pre-Islamic moon worship of Arabia. Mohammed was said to be of the Hashemite clan. This is the same family from which former King Hussein of Jordan traced his lineage.

Mohammed's father, Abdullah, died shortly before Mohammed was born. A description of his mother, Aminah, is helpful in understanding the kind of upbringing Mohammed had as a child.

Robert Morey explains, "Mohammed's mother, Aminah, was of an excitable nature and often claimed that she was visited by spirits, or *jinns*. She also at times claimed to have visions and religious experiences. Mohammed's mother was involved in what we today would call the "occult arts," and this basic orientation is thought by some scholars to have been inherited by her son."[13]

It was the custom of the Quraish tribe to give their infants to the local Bedouin women to be nursed. For this purpose, young Mohammed was given to a woman named Halima, who nursed him for several years. Halima returned Mohammed to his mother because Mohammed had fits or seizures, which made Halima believe he was demon possessed. His mother, Aminah, died when Mohammed was six years of age.[14]

Mohammed's grandfather (Ab al-Muttalik) cared for him for two years after the death of his mother. Ab al-Muttalik was a powerful leader in Mecca and a guardian of the Kaaba. He taught Mohammed the ceremonies and traditions associated with moon worship. When his grandfather also died, the child was raised by his uncle, Abu Talib.

When Mohammed was ten years of age, he started accompanying his uncle, a camel driver, on many journeys. Mohammed eventually became a camel driver himself.[15]

During his journeys with his uncle, Mohammed came into contact with Jews and Christians from whom he heard stories about the Bible, Judaism, and Christianity. Unfortunately, by this time, Christianity had become a lifeless religion with desert monasteries filled with statues of saints and other icons and relics that were objects of worship. This would certainly not give Mohammed a true representation of biblical Christianity.

At the age of 25 Mohammed went to work for a wealthy widow named Khadijah. Although Khadijah was 40 years of age and had been married twice, she proposed marriage to Mohammed and he accepted. Khadijah bore Mohammed six children, but only one, a daughter named Fatima, lived to maturity. Khadijah died at the age of 65. She had been Mohammed's only wife for 25 years.[16]

The Prophetic Seal

As an adult, Mohammed was about medium height and weight with heavy shoulders, long, thick, black curling hair and a long, bushy beard. He had a large forehead, and large black eyes that were often bloodshot. He seemed to be a restless person who walked very fast as if impatient to reach his destination. He was almost illiterate and of average intelligence.[17]

In pre-Islamic Arabia, moon worshipers, like many other pagans, believed their spiritual leaders were marked in some physical way by their gods as a sign of prophet hood. This may be like circumcision which marks Jewish males as the covenant people of God. This mark was a sign of the prophetic calling and a physical way the prophet could be identified.[18]

As explained below, the Meccans believed that the special sign or "seal" of their spiritual leader was a large hairy mole on his back, just below the neck.[19] Did Mohammed have such a sign on his body?

The Koran reads, "Mohammed is not the father of any of your men, but he is the apostle of Allah, and the Seal of the prophets: and Allah has full knowledge of all things."[20]

Robert Payne explains that the Arabs were attracted to Mohammed because he had a mole, the size of a pigeon's egg between his shoulders.[21] This was the most important aspect of his physical appearance because it was the sign pagan Arabs accepted as the mark of a *shaman*, a special spiritualist who could influence the gods to favor the people with health, prosperity, protection, fertility, etc. When the Arabs considered Mohammed's claims regarding his visions, they wanted to know if he had the seal on his body.[22] Traditional Islamic writings all agree that this hairy mole on the back of Mohammed was the sign of his apostle hood.

Robert Morey provides the following information in his informative publication, *By Their Moles Ye Shall Know Them*: [23]

"The early Hadith scholars are unanimous in their interpretation of the identity and significance of the "seal of the prophets" found in Surah 33:40. The greatest of all Hadith scholars, al-Bukhari tells us, 'I stood behind him (Mohammed) and saw the seal of the Prophethood between his shoulders, and it was like the *'Zir-al-Hijla'* (meaning the button of a small tent, but some say egg of a partridge"(Vol. 1, No 189,Vol. 4, No. 741).[24]

Morey quotes another version of the Hadith where Jabir b. Sammura reported, "I saw the seal on his back as it were a pigeon's egg" (Hadith, vol. IV, CMLXXIX, page 1251).[25]

In the same work, Abdulla b. Sarjis reported, "I went in after him and saw the Seal of Prophet hood between his shoulders on the left side of his shoulder having spots on it like moles" (Hadith, vol. IV, CMLXXIX, page 1251).[26]

Morey provides this additional documentation by early Islamic scholars who wrote the following statements about Mohammed and the prophetic seal:

"A mole of an unusual size on the Prophet's back, which is said to have been the divine seal which, according to the prediction of the Scriptures, marked Mohammed as the "Seal of the Prophets" (Khatimu n-Nabiyin).[27]

"It was a piece of flesh, very brilliant in appearance, and according to some traditions it had secretly inscribed within it, 'Allah is one and has no associate'" (Shaikh Abdu l-Haqq).[28]

"Mohammed said to Abu Ramsa, 'Come hither and touch my back.' Which he did, drawing his fingers over the prophetic seal, and behold! There was a collection of hairs upon the spot. When Abu Ramsa offered to remove it, Mohammed said, 'The physician thereof is He who placed it where it is' "(Muir, new edition, page 542).[29]

Morey notes that the *Dictionary of Islam* gives the following comment on the "Seal of Prophecy:" "This," says one, "was a protuberance on the Prophet's back the size and appearance of a pigeon's egg." It is said to have been the divine seal which, according to the predictions of the scriptures, marked Mohammed as the last of the Prophets. ...From the traditions it would seem to have been nothing more than a mole of unusual size (page 389).[30]

Mohammed's Revelations

There are certain advantages to being married to a wealthy woman such as Mohammed's marriage to Khadijah. Since Mohammed did not have to work a steady job, he was free to spend his time meditating and worshipping at the Kabah.

In the year A.D. 610, at the age of 40, Mohammed began to receive revelations about Allah. He was meditating in a cave when he heard a voice say, "Read [Recite] in the name of your Lord who created, created man from clots of blood. Read! Your Lord is the most bountiful One, who by the pen taught man what he did not know" (Surah 96:1-2).[31]

There are different views as to the degree that Mohammed could read and write. Those who believe Mohammed could not read say the voice told him to "recite" rather than read. Whatever the truth about Mohammed's literacy, he was concerned about the source of these revelations. He wondered if he was possessed by demon spirits called "Jinn" as his childhood nurse feared.[32]

Mohammed was in such agony that he was ready to throw himself off a cliff when the voice claiming to be Gabriel reassured him that he was Allah's messenger.[33] Arthur Jeffery explains, "Thereat I fell to my knees where I had been standing, and then with trembling limbs dragged myself along till I came in to Khadijah, saying: "Wrap ye me up! Wrap ye me up!" till the terror passed from me. Then later he [the spirit] came to me again and said: "O Mohammed, thou art Allah's Apostle," [which so disturbed me] that I was about to cast myself down from some high mountain cliff. But he appeared before me as I was about to do this, and said "O Mohammed, I am Gabriel, and thou art Allah's Apostle."[34]

Alfred Guillaume adds, "From the books of tradition we learn that the prophet was subject to ecstatic seizures. He is reported to have said that when inspiration came to him he felt as it were the painful sounding of a bell. Even in cold weather his forehead was bathed in sweat. On one occasion he called to his wife to wrap him in a veil. At other times visions came to him in sleep...in its early stages Mohammed's verses were couched in the Semitic form of mantic oracular utterance...Veiling of the head and the use of rhymed prose were mars of the Arabian soothsayer, while the feeling of physical violence and compulsion...the outward appearance of "possession"...seemed to the onlookers to indicate the madness of demonic possession."[35]

Dr. William Miller gives further information about the manner of Mohammed's revelations, "Sometimes Mohammed saw the angel Gabriel, sometimes he only heard a voice, and sometimes he heard the sound of a bell through which the words of the angel were brought to him. Sometimes the message came in a dream, and at other times it came in the thoughts of his mind. When revelation came to him, his whole frame would become agitated, and perspiration would pour down his face. He would often fall to the ground and foam at the mouth. The messages always came to him in the Arabic language, and Mohammed spoke the words that he received...Mohammed was convinced that the words which came to him were not his own, but the very Word of God, and he was only the reciter." [36]

Mohammed was still unsure of the source of the voice. He was afraid he was going mad. He hurried to Mecca to share his experience with Khadijah. Caner and Caner explain: "Then Allah's Apostle returned with the inspiration and with his heart beating severely. Then he went to Khadijah bint Khuwalid and said, "Cover me! Cover me!" They covered him till his fear was over and after that he told her everything that had happened and said, "I fear that something may happen to me." Khadijah replied, "Never! By Allah, Allah will never disgrace you. You keep good relations with your kith and kin, help the poor and the destitute, serve your guests generously and assist the deserving calamity-afflicted ones" (Hadith 1.1.13).[37]

Though his uncle Abu Talib thought Mohammed needed deliverance, Khadijah convinced Mohammed that his revelations were from God and that God was calling him to share his revelations with the world. Mohammed's revelations soon led him to conclude that Allah was the one true god above all the other gods. Khadijah was his first convert.

As just noted, Mohammed's revelations were often accompanied by violent seizures and foaming at the mouth. He would fall to the ground with sweat dripping from his forehead. He would go into a trancelike state when he received his revelations and then proclaim what he was told to his listeners. His mind was often tormented and he contemplated suicide. His countenance became fierce and stern as the voice demanded complete obedience to the revelations. [38]

Robert Morey puts this in the Arab cultural perspective: "What must be remembered is that in the Arab culture of Mohammed's day, epileptic seizures were interpreted as a religious sign of either demonic possession or divine visitation. Mohammed initially considered both opinions as possible interpretations of his experience. At first he worried about the possibility that he was demon possessed. This led him to attempt to commit suicide. But his devoted wife was able to stop him from committing suicide by persuading him that he was such a good man that he could not possibly be demon possessed."[39]

Mohammed began to preach his message to the Meccans who strongly resisted his condemnation of their idols. Their resistance was so strong that Mohammed compromised by declaring that the gods of the Meccans could serve as intercessors in his new religion.

Remember Allah's three daughters represented by the stars? They were the intercessors. But this presented Mohammed with a real problem. He was preaching that Allah could not possibly have any offspring so how could he have three daughter goddesses?

Robert Morey explains Mohammed's dilemma, "In order to appease his pagan family members and the members of the Quraish tribe, he decided that the best thing he could do was to agree with the tradition—that it was perfectly proper to pray to and worship the three daughters of Allah: Al-Lat, Al-Uzza and Manat.

"This led to the famous "satanic verses" in which Mohammed in a moment of weakness and supposedly under the inspiration of Satan (according to early Muslim authorities) succumbed to the temptation to appease the pagan mobs in Mecca. The literature on the "satanic verses" is so vast that an entire volume could be written just on this one issue. Every general and Islamic reference work, Muslim or Western, deals with it as well as all the biographies of Mohammed.

"The story of Mohammed's temporary appeasement of the pagans by allowing them their polytheism cannot be ignored or denied. It is a fact of history that is supported by all Middle East scholars, Western and Muslim."[40]

When Mohammed's new converts heard of this concession, they strongly rebuked Mohammed forcing him to recant this proclamation. Mohammed explained that it was not Allah who gave him this revelation but that satan had deceived him. He then announced that Allah could abrogate or cancel any previous revelation. This means that any later revelation written in the Koran cancels any previous revelation in the Koran.

As Mohammed gained followers, he became a threat to the Quraish elders and their system of worship. They forced him and his followers to flee to Medina which was two hundred and seventy miles to the North. His departure from Mecca on June 25 in the year A.D. 622 marks the beginning of the Muslim calendar.[41]

Mohammed was 53 years of age when he arrived in Medina. He was so well received that he soon became the city's political and spiritual leader. This is ironic because Medina was founded by Jews from Syria. Bernard Lewis provides the following information, "In the Arabian land considered by many to be "purely Arab," the land which would spawn Islam many centuries later, numbers of Jewish and Christian settlements were established in different parts of Arabia, both spreading Aramaic and Hellenistic culture. The chief southern Arabian Christian center was in Najran, where a relatively advanced political life was developed. Jews and Judaized Arabs were everywhere, especially in Yathrib later named Medina. They were mainly agriculturists and artisans."[42]

Guillaume adds the following about the Jewish presence in the area:

> At the dawn of Islam the Jews dominated the economic life of the Hijaz (the sacred eastern section of Arabia that contains Medina and Mecca). They held all of the best land...At Medina they must have formed at least half of the population. There was also a Jewish settlement to the north of the Gulf of Aqaba. What is important is to note that the Jews of the Hijaz made many proselytes (or converts) among the Arab tribesman.[43]

The Jews at Medina were looking for the Messiah. Mohammed tried to appeal to them by presenting himself as a follower of Abraham and the Messiah they were awaiting. He proclaimed that Allah had told him to pray toward Jerusalem three times as day as was the custom of the Jews. Now this is most interesting since the Arabs say the Jews have no historical claim on Jerusalem. If this is true, why did Mohammed try to appeal to them by praying toward Jerusalem? He also had his followers circumcised and recognized the Sabbath as a special holy day.[44]

The Jews initially favored Mohammed until they further examined his life and teachings. When they rejected him as a prophet of Abraham and Moses, Mohammed turned on them and others in nearby towns. He then reversed his proclamations that appealed to the Jews and replaced them with ones more acceptable to the Arabs.[45]

In one of his cruelest actions, Mohammed and his followers beheaded six to nine hundred Jewish men, sold the women and children as slaves, and confiscated their property. This was done in one day in the year 627. This event would change the course of history. Mohammed's would express his hate of the Jews from this time forward in the Koran. His successors have followed his example throughout history as is now seen in the Arab-Israeli conflict.

From the very beginning, Mohammed established "jihad" as the way to spread Islam. You either accepted his message or you were beheaded. Modern Islamic terrorists are following Mohammed's example when they behead their enemies. Mohammed then declared that Allah told him and the faithful to pray toward Mecca.[46]

In A.D. 628, Mohammed signed a ten-year peace treaty with the Quraish tribal leaders in Mecca which allowed him and his followers to make their annual pilgrimage to Mecca. Two years later (A.D. 630), when Mohammed had a large enough army, he broke the treaty and conquered Mecca in the name of Allah. He went to the Ka'bah, destroyed the idols, and pronounced, "There is no God but God (Allah); there is none with him." [47]

Modern Islamic terrorist organizations follow Mohammed's example when they make "peace agreements" with Israel. They have no intention of keeping the agreement. They use the lull in fighting to rearm. When they believe they are strong enough they renew their attacks against Israel.

Mohammed continued to receive his visions concerning Allah for the next 25 years. Convinced they were given to him by the angel Gabriel, He enforced his revelations with the sword. Any group that failed to submit was slaughtered.

Some would say that Mohammed used his revelations to justify his political, military and moral behavior. He conveniently received a revelation from Allah endorsing his intention whenever it suited his purpose to fight a battle, execute an enemy, annex territory, add a wife, etc.

For example, when seeing Zainab, the wife of his adopted son, unveiled, he sang out in a sudden burst of emotion, "Praise belongeth unto God who turneth the hearts of men even as he will." Later, Mohammed claimed that Allah had given him permission to marry Zainab.[48]

Mohammed had a total of 15 wives, including two who were Jewish and one who was a Christian. His youngest wife, Ayisha, said that her husband loved three things: women, scents, and food.[49]

On June 8, in A.D. 632, at the age of 62, Mohammed died and was buried at Medina. After his death, his followers recorded his revelations in the Koran.[50]

SPREADING THE MESSAGE

When Mohammed died, he was succeeded by four consecutive leaders. They are called, "Caliphs" which means successors. Later the word came to be used as a title of the person who became the religious and political leader after Mohammed.

About 20 years after Mohammed's death, the third Caliph, Uthman ibn Affan, wrote a revised edition of the sayings of Mohammed. He destroyed all previous versions and made his the final official version of the Koran.

Mohammed's successors used the sword to rapidly extend the influence of Islam. They had phenomenal success. In a short period of time, they conquered all of Arabia, the Middle East, North Africa, and parts of India.

With one victory after another, they extended their emerging empire into Europe with conquests of much of Spain and

Portugal. They advanced on France and were poised to bring "Christian Europe" under the rule of Islam. With their superior numbers and fanatical devotion, victory seemed certain. Yet, they were miraculously stopped by Charles Martel at the Battle of Tours in A.D. 732. They were only 100 miles from Paris.[51]

While the West developed politically, economically, socially and scientifically, Islam retreated and stagnated. Islam failed to keep up with the West because it was locked into a seventh century mindset.

Centuries later, Islam made another attempt to conquer Christian Europe for Allah. This time it was the Ottoman Turks who ruled the Middle East from 1517-1917. In the seventeenth century, the Turks sought to extend their empire into Europe. They conquered Constantinople in 1453 ending the one thousand year Eastern Christian Byzantine Empire. They renamed Constantinople calling it Istanbul and established it as the new capital of the Ottoman Empire.

They conquered parts of Eastern Europe and in 1683 threatened to overrun Austria. Once again, the fate of Christian Europe was at stake. With a huge army ready to invade Vienna, it seemed like a certain victory for the armies of Allah. As if by divine providence, the defenders of Vienna were victorious and stopped the advancing armies of the Turks.[52]

With this defeat, Islam once again retreated. As the Christian West continued to advance, Islam failed to progress and went into decline. The gap between the Christian and Islamic cultures and civilizations widened as the West prospered and Islam stagnated as it failed to breakout of its seventh century culture and mindset.

With the discovery of oil in Muslim countries, radical Islamists now have the financial means to attempt to conquer the West for Allah. The Ayatollah Khomeini was instrumental in sparking the modern Islamic revival that has spread throughout the Middle East and is threatening the world.

Because Islamic controlled countries have failed to prosper and advance, as has the West, they are jealous of America and Western democracies. They saw the American liberation of Iraq as another Crusade by the Christian West to dominate Islam. The Iraqi people don't know if America is their liberator or conqueror.

While they understood that Saddam Hussein was a ruthless dictator, they were humiliated that "Christian" America had to overthrow Saddam. Since they view Islam as superior to Judeo/Christianity, this was a terrible blow to their pride.

Even though the superior American military easily defeated Saddam Hussein, the battle for Iraq has just begun. Iran, who along with Iraq, is 90 percent Shiite, will continue to seek to influence the future or Iraq and attempt to establish a radical Islamic state. Islam sees Israel and America as its major enemies that must be subdued. This is a spiritual battle between the God of the Bible and the god of Islam. The destiny of the world and our way of life is at stake.

While there are challenging times ahead, the outcome of the conflict is certain. King Nebuchadnezzar of Babylon (modern day Iraq) recognized that the One True God rules over the nations and exercises His will as He pleases. Even though a pagan king, he praised the God of Abraham, Isaac, and Jacob with these words:

> And at the end of the time I, Nebuchadnezzar, lifted my eyes to heaven, and my understanding returned to me; and I blessed the Most High and praised and honored Him who lives forever: For His dominion is an everlasting dominion, and His kingdom is from generation to generation. All the inhabitants of the earth are reputed as nothing; He does according to His will in the army of heaven and among the inhabitants of the

earth. No one can restrain His hand or say to Him, "What have you done?"[54]

Personal Study Review

1. Explain pre-Islamic worship.
2. Describe the early life of Mohammed.
3. Give your views of Mohammed's revelations.
4. Explain how Islam was able to expand so fast in such a short period of time.

Chapter 4

Islam and Christianity

In a 2007 survey of 1,000 Muslims conducted by the leading Islamic organization in America, seventy seven percent said they believe that Muslims worship the same God as Christians and Jews.[1] I'm sure if a survey was taken of non-observant Jews and Christians, they would give the same answer. Most people don't know what their religion teaches.

Is the Allah of Islam the same as the Yahweh of the Bible? Do we all worship the same God but under different names? Are the teachings of Islam and the Koran compatible to the teachings of the Hebrew Bible, Christianity and the New Testament? What does the Koran say about Jesus? What does the Koran say about Jews and Christians? What is the source of the hatred radical Islamists have for "the infidels?" What does Islam teach about women? We will answer these questions in this chapter by comparing the actual words in the Koran with the Bible.

As we begin to see the contrast between Islam, Judaism and Christianity, it is important that the reader understand this comparison is not in any way intended to be anti-Arab or anti-Muslim. We are simply presenting what Islam teaches in relationship to Judeo-Christianity. Let's begin by answering the most important of all the questions, "Is the Allah of Islam the same as the Yahweh of the Bible?"

THE GOD OF ISLAM AND THE GOD OF THE BIBLE

Islam is a monotheistic religion in that it teaches belief in one god. In Islam, there is only one true god and his name is Allah. Allah is all-seeing, all-knowing, and all-powerful. This is the most important declaration of the Muslim faith.

The world believes that Jews, Christians and Muslims worship the same God but by a different name. As we will discover in this chapter, there is a great difference between the Muslim understanding of God and the Judeo-Christian understanding of God. But it is best if you make up your own mind about this. While Jews and Christians have theological differences, we worship the same God and share the same holy Book. Our differences are in matters of interpretation of the same book, not a different book.

The same cannot be said of Islam. There are many conflicts between the Bible and the Koran. Regardless of how one views the relationship between Judaism, Christianity and Islam, the revelation of Allah in the Koran is different than the revelation of Yahweh given in the Bible. The same deity cannot possibly be the author of both the Bible and the Koran. As we learned in the last chapter, Islam has its roots in pagan moon worship. Therefore, its founder, its theology and its holy book reflect a different understanding of the Creator than does Judeo-Christianity.

While the Koran says that Allah created man from clots of blood, the Bible says that God created man from the dust of the earth after His own image and likeness so that mankind could know God personally. Both versions cannot be correct. Creating from clots of blood is impersonal as opposed to being created in God's own image.

The Koran says: "Recite in the name of your Lord who created—created man from clots of blood."[2]

The Bible says:

> *Then God said, Let Us make man in Our image after Our likeness. So God created man in His own image.... And the Lord God formed man of the dust of the ground, and breathed into his nostrils the breath of life; and man became a living soul.*[3]

In reading the Koran, we soon realize that Allah is presented as a remote god who cannot be known personally. He is impersonal and unknowable. He is a stern god, full of judgment and power, but lacking the attributes of love, purity and grace. For example, the word "love" is mentioned only a few times in the Koran and only in a general conditional way. One simply cannot read the Koran and get the impression that Allah loves you.

The Koran says that Allah is merciful and compassionate. But when we finish reading the Koran, we do not have the sense of offering gratitude to Allah for his loving-kindness. Allah is to be obeyed and feared, not loved and known in a personal way. While we wish this was not true, wishful thinking does not make things true. This is the way Allah is presented in the Koran.

The God of the Bible is also to be feared (reverential respect) and obeyed. His greatness and majesty is far beyond human understanding. But in contrast to Allah, the God of the Bible loves us and wants us to know Him in a personal way. He has taken the initiative to make Himself known to us through creation, instinct, the Bible, and, for Christians, ultimately through Jesus of Nazareth.

In the Hebrew Bible, God proclaims, "The Lord did not set His love on you nor choose you because you were more in number than any other people, for you were the least of all peoples; but because the Lord loves you…."[4]

The New Testament tells us, "For God so loved the world that He gave His only begotten Son that whoever believes in Him should not perish but have everlasting life."[5]

Knowing God

The Bible says that God wants us to know Him. When the Bible speaks of knowing God it does not mean learning theological facts about God that we know in our head. Nor does it mean to have an intellectual awareness of God. It means to have an intimate relationship with Him.

This is a major difference between the Western, Greco-Roman understanding of knowledge and the biblical-Hebraic understanding of knowing God. To know God in the biblical sense is to experience Him, to fellowship with Him, and to walk with Him. It is also the major difference between the Islamic concept of God and that of Judeo-Christianity.

In the Hebrew Bible, Jeremiah explains:

> Thus says the Lord: Let not the wise man glory in his wisdom, let not the mighty man glory in his might, nor let the rich man glory in his riches; but let him who glories glory in this, that he understands and knows Me, that I am the Lord exercising loving-kindness, judgment, and righteousness in the earth. For in these things I delight, says the Lord.[6]

The New Testament adds these words:

And this is eternal life, that they may know You, the only true God, and Jesus Christ whom You have sent."[7]

While the God of the Bible hates sin, He loves the sinner. God's love is a holy love that flows out of His being. It is not like human love that is sentimental or based on the object of His love. He must judge sin, but He also extends His love and desires to be loved in return. He tempers His righteous anger with His grace, mercy, and forgiveness. Without a clear biblical revelation and personal experience of the love and forgiveness of God, we humans would be so terrified of God; we would never want to know Him.

God as Father

In the Bible, God presents Himself as a loving "Heavenly Father." Many people do not have a good relationship with their father. They project their negative earthly experience toward God. They are afraid of God. But as a good human father provides love, guidance and protection to his children, so the God of the Bible gives perfect love, protection and guidance to His children.

How does this biblical revelation of God as "Father" compare to the revelation of Allah in the Koran? The word "Father," which implies a guiding and loving relationship, is not mentioned even once in the Koran. Of the 99 attributes of Allah in the Koran, "Father" is not one of them. One cannot know Allah as father because this would suggest that Allah has children. Remember Allah's daughters? In the mind of Islam, for Allah to have children means he must have sexual relations with some other god or with humans. Mohammed had to recant that accommodation. This is a blasphemous thought to Islam, as well as to Jews and Christians.

When we speak of God as "Father" we speak of the relationship we can have with Him, not that God gave birth to us in some sex act with other gods or with humans. We are God's offspring through creation and, in the spiritual sense, through redemption.

In contrast to the Allah of Islam, Judeo-Christianity both understands God as Father. The Hebrew Bible and the New Testament both present God in this way. The Hebrews understood God as their Father as we see in the prayer of King David, "Blessed are You, Lord God of Israel, our Father, forever and ever."[8]

The New Testament also presents God as Father. Jesus said:

> And when you pray, do not use vain repetitions as the heathen do, for they think they will be heard for their many words. Therefore, do not be like them. For your Father knows the things you have need of before you ask Him. In this manner, therefore, pray: Our Father in heaven, hallowed be Your name.[9]

WHAT IS GOD'S NAME?

In ancient times, gods and people were known by their names. The name told about the nature and character of the god or person. There were many national and local gods, and they all had names. The name identified the god that one worshiped.

In the Bible, God is known by His name. When God called Moses to lead the Hebrews out of Egypt, the one thing Moses wanted to know was God's name. Exodus reads,

> Then Moses said to God, "Indeed when I come to the children of Israel and say to them, The God of your fathers has sent me to you, and they say to me, 'What is His name?' What shall I say to them?" And God said to Moses, "I AM WHO I AM." And He said, "Thus you shall say to the children of Israel, 'I AM has sent me to you.'" Moreover God said to Moses...

> "This *is* My name forever, and this *is* My memorial to all generations."[10]

God revealed His name to be, "I AM." *I AM* means "to be" or more technically, the self-existing, uncaused One who was, who is, and who is to come. His name in Hebrew is represented in English by the four constants, YHWH. It is spelled out in English as Yahweh. He is not the god of the son or the moon or the Sumerians, the Babylonians, Persians, Egyptians, etc. He is the one true God who had identified Himself by His name. He said this was His name forever.

God's highest motivation is to see that His name is honored and revered by mankind. If for no other reason, God must keep His covenant promises and commitments revealed in the Bible or He is not the true God. We are to honor God's name, give thanks to God's name, exalt His name, bless His name, fear His name, praise His name, be jealous for His name, etc. There are many references to this in the Hebrew Bible. The writer of Psalms said, "Give unto the Lord the glory due His name...."[11]

In the New Testament, Jesus said that He made known God's name: "I have manifested Your name to the men whom You have given me out of the world...keep through Your name, those whom You have given Me...I have declared to them Your name...."[12]

The god of Islam does not have a name. The word "Allah" simply means God or "the God." When Moslem worshipers declare that, "Allah is God," they are simply saying, "god is god," or "the god is god." When the spirit claiming to be Gabriel gave revelations to Mohammed, it did not reveal which god it was representing. It did not give the name of the deity. The god of Islam did not identify itself as the God of Abraham, Isaac, and Jacob.

The God of the Bible declared that He was the One True God and there is no other, "Remember the former things of old; for I am God, and there is no other...."[13]

"Thus says the Lord, the King of Israel and His Redeemer, the Lord of hosts: I am the first and I am the last; besides Me there is no god. And who can proclaim as I do?..."[14]

"O Lord, there is none like You, nor is there any God besides You, according to all that we have heard with our ears. And who is like Your people Israel, the one nation on the earth whom God went to redeem for Himself as a people-to make for Yourself a name...?"[15]

Is the Yahweh of the Bible the same as the Allah of the Koran? We have asked this question several times previously. And by now you may have already formed an opinion. Regardless of statements made by political and religious leaders, Christian, Jew and Muslim, and regardless of what we might like to think, let's let the Koran speak for itself.

"Say: Unbelievers (Jews and Christians), I do not worship what you worship, nor do you worship what I worship. I shall never worship what you worship, nor will you ever worship what I worship. You have your own religion, and I have mine."[16]

THE KORAN AND THE BIBLE

The Bible claims to be the written revelation of the one true God. Both divisions of the Bible tell us that the Scriptures were given to mankind by God. We read in the Hebrew Bible:

> "So Moses came down and told the people all the words of the Lord and all the judgments. And all the people answered with one voice and said, "All the words which the Lord has said we will do." And Moses wrote all the words of the Lord...Then he took the Book of the Covenant and read it in the hearing of the people. And they said, "All that the Lord has said we will do, and be obedient." And Moses took the blood, sprinkled it on the people,

> and said, "This is the blood of the covenant which the Lord has made with you according to all these words." [17]

The New Testament makes the same claim:

"All Scripture is given by inspiration of God, and is profitable for doctrine, for reproof, for correction, for instruction in righteousness, that the man of God may be complete, thoroughly equipped for every good work."[18]

Unlike the private interpretation Mohammed claimed to receive from Gabriel, the New Testament is clear that the biblical revelation was given to many by God's own Spirit: "Knowing this first, that no prophecy of Scripture is of any private interpretation, for prophecy never came by the will of man, but holy men of God spoke as they were moved by the Holy Spirit."[19]

The Bible was written over a 1,600-year period. Over 40 writers recorded the story, yet they tell it with perfect unity and harmony. They tell the story in three languages (Hebrew, Aramaic, and Greek), and on three continents (Asia, Africa, and Europe).

The writers of the Bible were separated by language, culture, geography, and other factors, writing on many controversial subjects. Nonetheless, they tell the same story. This is impossible unless God was helping them, whispering in their ear the same story.

The Bible is the most reliably preserved book of all ancient manuscripts. This is not just my opinion. It is a fact that anyone can investigate. God said He would preserve His Word, and He certainly has done this in spite of many efforts down through the ages to destroy it.

Although many people question the Bible's inspiration, no one who has studied the history of the Bible can seriously challenge its reliability. If a person disclaims the Bible from an intellectual viewpoint, he must also disclaim every ancient document which has ever been written, because the Bible is the most authenticated and reliable of all ancient books. You can bet your life on the words of the Bible. Yet, with no historical support, Mohammed challenged the integrity and reliability of the Bible. He said it had been corrupted by the "People of the Book," first the Jews and then the Christians.

The basic teaching in Islam is that the Bible, in its original form, was given by Allah and that all the true prophets in the Bible are Muslims. Over time, the Jews and Christians falsified the biblical record. The Koran has replaced the Bible as the true written record from God. The Gospels were changed to present Jesus differently than the original revelation supposedly given by Allah to the Jews and Christians. Furthermore, Mohammed taught that Jews and Christians deleted portions from the Bible that spoke of Mohammed and Islam.

This is how Mohammed explained the many discrepancies between the Bible and the Koran. Without any proof, He simply claimed that the Bible had been corrupted, and he now had the true revelation. Yet, no scholar can point to a time in history when this supposed corruption took place. Should we accept the word of a single man in a cave who many thought was demon possessed over the test of proven history? The Koran makes the following statements about the Bible.

"When they are told: Believe in what Allah has revealed, they reply: We believe in what was revealed to us. But they deny what has since been revealed, although it is the truth, corroborating their own scriptures."[20]

> "But because they broke their covenant, we laid on them our curse and hardened their hearts. They have tampered with words out of their context and forgotten much of what they were enjoined. With those who said they were Christians, we made a covenant also, but they too have forgotten much of what they

> were enjoined. People of the Book! Our apostle has come to reveal to you much of what you have hidden of the Scriptures..."[21]

Whereas the Bible says that Abraham offered Isaac as a sacrifice to God on Mt. Moriah, the Koran says that Abraham built the shrine to Allah in Mecca and offered Ishmael as the sacrifice.

"Make the place where Abraham stood a house of worship. We enjoined Abraham and Ishmael to cleanse our House for those who walk around it. ...Abraham and Ishmael built the House and dedicated it..."[22]

In The Ranks, verses 100-112, the Koran clearly implies that Abraham offered his son as a sacrifice at Mecca. While it doesn't name the son, Isaac is listed separate from the son. This can only mean that the Koran teaches that Abraham offered Ishmael in Mecca, not Isaac in Jerusalem.

Jesus promised that He would send the Holy Spirit who would be our helper, teacher, guide, etc. Islam claims that Jesus was speaking about Mohammed.

"And of Jesus the son of Mary, who said to the Israelites, I am sent forth to you from Allah to confirm the Torah already revealed, and to give news of an apostle that will come after me who name is Ahmad..."[23]

Ahmad is another name from Mohammed, meaning "The Praised One." He claimed the Jews and Christians corrupted the text so it would not speak of Mohammed as the "comforter."

There are so many other discrepancies between the Koran and the Bible it is not possible to reconcile them. The point is that since Islam teaches the Bible is a corrupted book superseded by the Koran, Jews and Christians really have no basis for discussing their differences with Muslims. Muslims do not accept the Bible as trustworthy.

ISLAM AND JESUS

Christians are more interested in what the Koran says about Jesus than any other subject. The Hebrew Bible says that God has a Son.

> *For unto us a Child is born, unto us a Son is given: and the government will be upon His shoulder. And His name will be called Wonderful, Counselor, Mighty God, Everlasting Father, Prince of Peace. Of the increase of His government there will be no end, upon the throne of David and over His kingdom, to order it and establish it with judgment and justice from that time forward, even forevermore. The zeal of the Lord of hosts will perform this.*[24]

"Who has ascended into heaven, or descended? Who has gathered the wind in His fists? Who has bound the waters in a garment? Who has established all the ends of the earth? What is His name, and what is His Son's name, if you know?"[25]

"You are My Son, today I have begotten You."[26]

In the New Testament, Jesus is presented as that Son who died for our sins, rose from the dead and will return to earth to establish the Kingdom of God on the earth. When Jesus was baptized, the voice of God proclaimed, "This is My beloved Son, in whom I am well pleased."[27]

While the Koran says many positive things about Jesus, including His virgin birth and return to earth, His miracles and anointing by the Holy Spirit, it claims His followers corrupted the original text about Jesus. The Jesus of the Koran is a different Jesus than the Jesus of the New Testament.

The Koran puts Arab desert clothes on Jesus and makes Him an apostle and prophet of Allah. The Koran denies the basic core teachings of the Gospel concerning the person of Jesus and His work of redemption. The Koran denies that Jesus is the Son of

God. It denies that He was crucified for our sins. It denies that He was resurrected.

"Say: Allah is One, the Eternal God. He begot none, nor was He begotten. None is equal to Him"[28]

"Say: If the Lord of Mercy had a son, I would be the first to worship him"[29]

"Unbelievers are those who say: Allah is the Messiah, the son of Mary…Unbelievers are those that say: God is one of three…."[30]

"The Messiah, the son of Mary, was no more than an apostle…."[31]

"People of the Book, do not transgress the bounds of your religion. Speak nothing but the truth about Allah. The Messiah, Jesus the son of Mary, was no more than Allah's apostle and His Word which he cast to Mary: a spirit from Him. So believe in Allah and His apostles and do not say: Three. Forbear and it shall be better for you. Allah is but one God. God forbid that he should have a son."[32]

"Say: Praise be to Allah who has never begotten a son; who has no partner in His Kingdom…."[33]

They denied the truth and uttered a monstrous falsehood against Mary. They declared: We have put to death the Messiah, Jesus the son of Mary, the apostle of Allah. They did not kill him, nor did they crucify him, but thought they did. Those that disagreed about him were in doubt concerning him; they knew nothing about him that was not sheer conjecture; they did not slay him for certain. Allah lifted him up.[34]

Islam teaches that Jesus will return at the end of the age and explain to Christians that they were wrong to honor Him as the Son of God. Jesus will convert everyone to Islam and destroy those who refuse to convert. Jesus will marry and eventually die and be buried in Mecca next to Mohammed. There will be a great war, a resurrection and judgment which will usher in a period of Islamic paradise on the earth.

JIHAD IN THE KORAN

Initially, Mohammed spoke kindly toward Jews and Christians. He even called the Jews God's chosen people and acknowledged that God gave them the Promised Land. He said that Jews and Christians should not be forced to accept Islam. But when they did not accept him as a true prophet of Abraham, he turned against them. Unfortunately, Mohammed taught and practiced violence from the very beginning.

When you read the following verses in the Koran, you will notice how Mohammed's revelations change from conciliatory to confrontational. While Muslim leaders are quick to point out the conciliatory statements, they fail to mention the change to confrontational.

As we learned in the previous chapter, Mohammed's later revelations superceded all earlier revelations. The statement in the Koran is clear, "If we supercede any verse or cause it to be forgotten, we bring a better one or one similar. Do you not know that Allah has the power over all things?"[35]

The following statements are very conciliatory.

"Children of Israel, remember the favor I have bestowed upon you, and that I exalted you above the nations."[36]

"Bear in mind the words of Moses to his people. He said: Remember, my people, the favor Allah has bestowed upon you. He has raise up prophets among you, made you kings, and given you that which He has given to no other nation. Enter my people, the holy land which Allah has assigned for you ..."[37]

"We gave the Book to the Israelites and bestowed on them wisdom and prophethood. We proved them with good things and exalted them above the nations...."[38]

"Believers, Jews, Christians, and Sabaeans—whoever believes in Allah and the Last Day and does what is right—shall be rewarded by their Lord; they have nothing to fear or to regret."[39]

"There shall be not compulsion in religion."[40]

Now notice how Allah has changed His mind. He says something totally opposite. He is now confrontational. He now says that his followers are to kill the infidels. Like it or not, this is simply Mohammed's own change in attitude toward the Jews and Christians which he attributed to Allah. We are toward that Islam is a religion of peace. This does not sound like a peaceful religion. But you decide for yourself.

"Fighting is obligatory for you...."[41]

"Slay them wherever you find them. ...Fight against them until idolatry is no more and Allah's religion reigns supreme."[42]

"Believers do not make friends with any but your own people...."[43]

"We will put terror in the hearts of the unbelievers...."[44]

"The true believers fight for the cause of Allah, but the infidels fight for the cause of the devil. Fight then against the friends of Satan...."[45]

"The only reward of those who make war upon Allah and His messenger and strive after corruption in the land will be that they will be killed or crucified, or have their hands and feet on alternative sides cut off, or will be expelled from the land."[46]

"...Beware of them lest they seduce you from some part of that which Allah has revealed to you. And if they turn away know that Allah's will is to smite them."[47]

"Believers, take neither the Jews nor the Christians for your friends...."[48]

"Allah revealed His will to the angels, saying, 'I shall be with you. Give courage to the believers. I shall cast terror into the hearts of the infidels. Strike off their heads, Strike off the very tips of their fingers.' Let not the unbelievers think that they will ever get away. They have not the power to do so. Muster against them all the men and cavalry at your command, so that you may strike terror into the enemy of Allah and your enemy."[49]

"...Slay the idolaters wherever you find them, and take them captive, and besiege them, and prepare to ambush them."[50]

Mohammed's sanctioning of jihad in the Koran was carried over into the Hadith and other Muslim books that record the acts and sayings of Mohammed. Mohammed taught that the end of days and the resurrection of the dead would not come until the Muslims killed all the Jews. There would be such hatred against the Jews that even the trees and rocks would cry out against them. They would tell Muslims if a Jew was hiding behind it and beckon the Muslim to come and kill the Jew.

The Hadith reads, "The last hour will not come unless the Muslims will fight against the Jews and the Muslims would kill them until the Jews would hide themselves behind a stone or tree and a stone or a tree would say: 'Muslim, or the servant of Allah, there is a Jew behind me; come and kill him....'"[51]

Now let us reason together for a moment. Would God say in the Bible that the Jews are His chosen people with an everlasting covenant and then say in the Koran to kill all the Jews? How can this be the same God?

Caner and Caner make the following observation regarding the violent nature of Islam:

With the notable exception of the Crusades, Muslims have initiated almost all wars, due largely to the philosophy of jihad. War is not a sidebar of history for Islam; it is the main vehicle for religious expansion. It is the Muslim duty to bring world peace via the sword. Conservative Muslims see Western culture as destructive to Islamic traditions and beliefs. While modern people are familiar only with the defensive Islam of the last three hundred years, the religion has never forgotten the previous one thousand years of conquest in the cause of Allah. It is this traditional conquering Islam that has reemerged.[52]

The Koran and Women

While the Judeo-Christian tradition emphasizes equality of women, the Koran and the Hadith, have a much different view of women. Regardless of how Islam claims that it holds women in high regard, Islamic holy books say different. Some of the statements in the Koran and Hadith are listed below. They are very clear and don't require any comment. Any Western woman can understand the meaning of the texts.

1. ***Men are Superior to Women***

   "Women shall with justice have rights similar to those exercised against them, although men have a status above women."[53]

2. ***Men have Authority over Women to Beat Them***

   "Men have authority over women because Allah had made the one superior to the other, and because they spend their wealth to maintain them. Good women are obedient. They guard their unseen parts because Allah has guarded them. As for those from who you fear disobedience, admonish them and send them to beds apart and beat them. Then if they obey you, take no further action against them. Allah is high, supreme."[54]

As I was writing this, an article appeared in the news about a court case in Germany. A Muslim woman was seeking a divorce in a German court on the basis that her Muslim husband was beating her. The judge ruled against the woman and cited this text in the Koran as the basis for his judgment. While the more enlightened Muslims in the community protested the decision, the point is that the judge recognized that the Koran sanctions "wife beating."

3. *Women Receive half the Inheritance of Men*

   "A male shall inherit twice as much as a female."[55]

4. *A Woman's Witness is Worth Half that of a Man*

   "Call in two male witnesses from among you, but if two men cannot be found, then one man and two women whom you judge fit to act as witnesses."[56]

5. *A Wife is Considered a Possession*

   "Men are tempted by the lure of women and offspring, of hoarded treasures of gold and silver, of splendid horses, cattle, and plantations."[57]

6. *Men May Marry Four Wives at One Time*

   "If you fear you cannot treat orphans with fairness, then you may marry other women who seem good to you: two, three, or four of them."[58]

7. *Women are to Veil Themselves when Outside the Home*

   "Prophet, enjoin your wives, your daughters, and the wives of true believers to draw their veils close round them …."[59]

8. *Women are Considered Sex Objects*

   "Women are your fields; go, then, into your fields whence you please."[60]

"Wives are playthings, so take your pick."[61]

9. ***Men May Divorce Women by a Simple Oral Announcement***

   "Divorce may be pronounced twice, and then a woman must be retained in honor or allowed to go with kindness."[62]

10. ***Women are Genetically Inferior to Men and Deficient in Mind***

    "According to Hadith 3.826, Mohammed said the women are genetically and legally inferior to men. ...This is because of the deficiency of the woman's mind."[63]

11. ***The Majority of People in Hell are Women***

    When Mohammed was shown a vision of hell, he said that the majority of its dwellers are women.[64]

12. ***Men May Divorce Their Wives Because of Sex***

    According to the Koran, men may divorce their wives if they are not meeting his sexual needs, "It may well be, that if he divorce you, his Lord (Allah) will give him in your place better wives than yourself."[65]

Irreconcilable Differences

I wish it was true that we all worshipped the same God and had the common motive of loving and serving our fellowman. Unfortunately, that is not the world in which we live. Jews and Christians have theological differences. But we worship the same God and share the same holy book. We are also share a common destiny and are looking for the Messiah. We cannot say the same for Islam.

The Koran presents a different deity than what we find in the Bible. Allah is a distant stern god who cannot be known. The

God of the Bible is a loving heavenly Father. While He is holy and hates sin, He loves the sinner and desires that we draw close to Him and know Him in a personal way.

Whenever Islam has been strong, it has attempted to spread its beliefs and way of life through the sword. With its great wealth from oil, it is once again threatening Judeo-Christianity. While there are perilous times ahead, "People of the Book" (Jews and Christians) have the assurance from the Bible that the day will come when the One True God will be King over all the earth. In that day, it shall be said that the Lord is one and His name one.[66]

Personal Study Review

1. Explain the difference between the god of Islam and the God of the Bible.
2. What does the Koran say about the Bible and why do you think it makes its claim?
3. What is the significance of God's name?
4. How does the teaching about Jesus in the Koran differ from the New Testament?
5. What is the source of radical Islamic jihad?

Chapter 5

ISLAM AND ISRAEL

The conflict between Islam and Israel began around the year 2000 B.C. The history of this family feud can be traced through the Book of Genesis. The God of the Bible promised that He would give a man named Abraham a land and make his descendants a great nation that would bless the whole world.

> *Now the Lord had said to Abram: Get out of your country, from your family and from your father's house, to a land that I will show you. I will make you a great nation; I will bless you and make your name great; and you shall be a blessing. I will bless those who bless you, and I will curse him who curses you; and in you all the families of the earth shall be blessed.*[1]

ABRAHAM WHAT HAVE YOU DONE?

God also promised to give Abraham a son as heir to the promises. When God spoke these things to Abraham, he was 85 years of age and his wife, Sarah, who was elderly, had never conceived.

It was the custom in those times for a barren woman to offer her bondwoman or slave to her husband in the hope that she might bear them a son. The child would be considered the offspring of the barren woman. Sarah, despairing of her age and infertility, did just that. She offered Abraham her Egyptian slave named Hagar. Abraham accepted Sarah's proposal and soon Hagar conceived and gave birth to a son. He was called Ishmael.

Ishmael is described in Genesis as a "wild man" whose hand would be against every man. The angel of the Lord says to Hagar:

> *Behold you are with child, and you shall bear a son. You shall call his name Ishmael, because the Lord has heard your affliction. He shall be a wild man; his hand shall be against every man, and every man's hand against him. And he shall dwell in the presence of all his brethren.*[2]

The Arabs consider Ishmael to be their father, but their earliest genealogy can be found in Genesis Chapter Ten. In this chapter we learn that Shem had a grandson named Eber. Eber had two sons: Peleg and Joktan. Based on the names of their descendants and the geographic locations where they lived, we understand that Peleg was the ancestor of the Jews and Joktan the ancestor of the Arabs. (See Genesis 10:22-32.)

God promised to bless Ishmael (Genesis 17:20) but He made it clear to Abraham that the heir to His promises would be a son born to Sarah. God supernaturally enabled Sarah to conceive, and she also gave birth to a son, which she named, Isaac. God made what the Bible describes as an everlasting covenant with Abraham. In this covenant, God promised to give the land of Canaan to Isaac (not Ishmael) and his descendants.

"And I will establish My covenant Between Me and you and your descendants after you in their generations, for an everlasting covenant, to be God to you and your descendants after you. Also I give to you and your descendants after you the land in which you are a stranger, all the land of Canaan, as an everlasting possession; and I will be their God."[3]

> And Abraham said to God, "Oh, that Ishmael might live before You!" Then God said: "No, Sarah your wife shall bear you a son, and you shall call his name Isaac; and I will establish My covenant with him for an everlasting covenant and with his descendants after him. And as for Ishmael, I have heard you. Behold, I have blessed him, and will make him fruitful, and will multiply him exceedingly. He shall beget twelve princes, and I will make him a great nation. But My covenant I will establish with Isaac, whom Sarah shall bear to you at this set time next year.[4]

God made provisions for both sons, but He established His covenant with Isaac, not Ishmael. He had different plans and purposes for Isaac and Ishmael as they would father different people groups. The Bible and the Koran cannot both correct regarding the covenant promise. It has to be one or the other.

This covenant promise God made to Abraham is still in effect today. This is the background to the conflict between these two sons of Abraham and their descendants that continues to this day. It is a story of conquest and conflict. While the Bible says that God made the covenant promise to Isaac and his descendants, the Koran says the promise was to Ishmael and his descendants. Both versions cannot be correct.

Brother Against Brother

Isaac married a woman chosen by his father. Her name was Rebecca. Rebecca bore twin sons named Jacob and Esau. According to the Bible, God selected Jacob as heir to the promises He had made to Abraham and Isaac. God later renamed Jacob and called him, Israel.

Jacob dreamed about a ladder reaching from earth to heaven. The Lord stood above the ladder and spoke to Jacob the promised blessing He had given to Abraham and Isaac.

> *And behold, the Lord stood above it and said: I am the Lord God of Abraham your father and the God of Isaac; the land on which you lie I will give to you and your descendants. Also your descendants shall be as the dust of the earth; you shall spread abroad to the west and the east, to the north and the south, and in you and in your seed all the families of the earth shall be blessed. Behold, I am with you and will keep you wherever you go, and will bring you back to this land; for I will not leave you until I have done what I have spoken to you.*[5]

While Isaac married a woman chosen by his father, Ishmael married an Egyptian woman who bore him twelve sons. Ishmael and his family moved to the geographic region now populated by the Arab people of Jordan and Saudi Arabia.

"So God was with the lad (Ishmael); and he grew and dwelt in the wilderness, and became an archer. He dwelt in the Wilderness of Paran; and his mother took a wife for him from the land of Egypt."[6]

"They dwelt from Havilah as far as Shur, which is east of Egypt as you go toward Assyria. He (Ishmael) died in the presence of his brethren."[7]

Jacob's twin brother Esau had a number of wives, one of which was the daughter of his Uncle Ishmael. Later, Esau took his family and settled near his Uncle Ishmael and his family.

"So Esau went to Ishmael and took Mahalath the daughter of Ishmael, Abraham's son, the sister of Nebajoth, to be his wife in addition to the wives he had."[8]

"Then Esau took his wives, his sons, his daughters, and all the persons of his household, his cattle and all his animals, and all his goods which he had gained in the land of Canaan, and went to a country away from the presence of his brother Jacob. So Esau dwelt in Mount Seir. Esau is Edom. And this is the genealogy of Esau the father of the Edomites in Mount Seir."[9]

Isaac spoke a blessing over his son, Esau. However, he also made the following interesting statement to Esau which has caused envy, jealousy, and fighting between the descendants of Esau (Arabs) and Jacob (Jews) throughout history, "By your sword you shall live, and you shall serve your brother..."[10]

Abraham's nephew, Lot, was the man God rescued from the destruction of Sodom. Lot had sons by his own daughters. Their children settled in land east of the Jordan River, as well as other parts of the modern Arab world.

Lot's firstborn son was called Moab. He was the father of the Moabites. The second son was named Ben-Ammi. He was the father of the Ammonites (Genesis 19). The Moabites and Ammonites became bitter enemies of the descendants of the children of Israel. Ancient Moab and Ammon are located in the geographic area known today as Jordan.

Abraham took another wife after Sarah died. Her name was Keturah. She bore Abraham six sons. Not wanting to make family matters worse, Abraham gave gifts to these sons and sent them away to live near Esau.

"But Abraham gave gifts to the sons of the concubines which Abraham had; and while he was still living he sent them eastward, away from Isaac his son, to the country of the east."[11]

These descendants of Abraham are the fathers of the modern Arab people. We learn from the Hebrew Bible and from secular history that animosity has continued between the two groups of family members from generation to generation. We learn also that because of their thirst for blood, the Arabs would have a history of violence and bloodshed which finds its religious expression in Islam.

"Because you have had an ancient hatred, and have shed the blood of the children of Israel by the power of the sword at the time of their calamity, when their iniquity came to an end, therefore, as I live says the Lord God, I will prepare you for blood, and blood shall pursue you; since you have not hated blood, therefore blood shall pursue you."[12]

Because of their hatred of God's chosen people, the Lord pronounces curses on the descendants of Ammon, Moab and Edom, as well as other nations in the Middle East that seek to destroy the people of God. (See Ezekiel 25-30.)

Psalm 83 clearly reveals the attitudes and purposes of the descendants of Ishmael and Esau (the Arab countries of our time) regarding their cousins, the present day descendants of Isaac and Jacob, who now make up the modern nation of Israel. This alarming Scripture sounds strangely familiar to the covenant made by the terrorists and the Arab nations concerning Israel. It reads as follows:

"...Come, and let us cut them [Israel] off from being a nation, that the name of Israel may be remembered no more. For they have consulted together with one consent; they form a confederacy against You [God]: who said, Let us take for ourselves the pastures of God for a possession."[13]

HOUSE OF PEACE—HOUSE OF WAR

The Arab-Israeli conflict is more than a family feud. It is a religious or spiritual battle. Islam cannot accept Israel as a neighbor because of the Islamic concept of relations between neighbors.

According to Islam, all nations controlled by Moslems are part of the "House of Peace." All others make up the "House of

War." Once Islam controlled a territory, Muslims consider it to be Islamic permanently. If the territory is lost to Islam, Allah has been diminished and the territory must be retaken.

Because the land of Israel was, at various times, ruled by Islam, Muslims feel that it must be recovered for the glory of Allah. This is the heart of the Arab-Israeli-Palestinian conflict.

In Islamic tradition, Allah's kingdom will not be established until the Muslims kill all the Jews and/or subject them to Muslim rule. The same attitude exists toward Christianity. This is why Muslim religious leaders incite mobs to murder in the name of Allah. When a Muslim kills a Jew, he shouts, "Allah Akbhar," meaning, "Allah is Great."

The Islamic "holy war" is aimed at Christians as well as Jews and all other religions. They also shout, "Today we kill the Saturday people (Jews), and tomorrow we kill the Sunday people (Christians.) This means that they first intend to destroy Israel and then establish Islamic rule over all that nations that subscribe to Christianity.

Western Naiveté

Failing to understand the nature of this conflict, the Western media paints Israel as unreasonable and stubborn. If only Israel would relinquish the West Bank to the PLO for the purpose of establishing a Palestinian state, there would be peace. It is terrible naïve for leaders of the West to think that such a concession would ever enable Israel and the Arab Islamic nations to settle their differences. The Arab nations will never agree to a real peace as long as "one inch" of territory is in Israeli hands and not in Allah's control.

The PLO has stated that the establishment of a Palestinian state is just the first stage of its plan to destroy Israel and recapture the territory for the glory of Allah. In fact, a Palestinian state has already been established. It is called Jordan.

When the newly formed League of Nations agreed to the establishment of the State of Israel, they divided the land into two states. The land west of the Jordan River was allocated to Jews and called Israel. The land east of the Jordan River was allocated to Arabs and called *Trans-Jordan*, meaning, across the Jordan River. Later the name of this Palestinian Arab country was simply called, Jordan.

Westerners, unaware of the religious and political history of these nations, are easily confused. However, Israel and the Arab Islamic countries understand perfectly what is at stake.

WHO ARE THE PALESTINIANS

According to the PLO (and the Western media), the Palestinian Arabs have lived in "Palestine" from time immemorial. They were forced to flee by the "Jewish Zionists" when the modern State of Israel was created. However, let's look at the facts.

Although the Jews were scattered among the nations by the Romans in a.d. 70, there has always been a Jewish presence in the land. The dream of the Jews in exile since their dispersion has been, "Next year in Jerusalem."

It was the Romans who renamed the land of Israel after the Jews' ancient enemy, the Philistines. They called it—Palestine.

Islamic rulers did dominate the Middle East for centuries. However, these rulers for the most part, were non-Arabs. During Arab domination of Palestine, the land was a neglected wasteland. It was sparsely populated by Jews and Arab peasants.

Jerusalem was never considered a sacred city to Islam and is not once even mentioned in the Koran. There has never been a sovereign, independent Palestinian or Arab state in the holy land from the time the Jews were dispersed until they declared their statehood in 1948. God has kept His covenant with word to Abraham by holding the land in trust all these centuries for the Jews.

The revival of modern Jewish life began in the late 1800s with the arrival of refugees from Russia and Eastern Europe. Later waves of immigration brought more Jews to their ancient land.

When the Jews arrived, they were greeted by a harsh land that had been neglected for centuries by its non-Arab Islamic rulers. Yet, these zealous Jewish immigrants were determined to redeem the soil.

As the Jews worked the land, it slowly began to prosper. The result was that thousands of Arab and non-Arab peasants from the neighboring countries came to Palestine as migrant farm workers. These migrant farm workers are the "Palestinians." They have not been in the land from "time immemorial." They are late arrivals who came to the land after it began to prosper as a result of Jewish blood and toil.

When Israel became a nation, 800,000 Jewish refugees fled from the neighboring Arab and Muslim states to Israel. They were all assimilated in the new state and became citizens of Israel.

The growing Arab Palestinian population was not as fortunate. Arab leaders from the neighboring countries declared war against Israel. They then instructed the Arab Palestinians to flee the Jewish state until the Jews were annihilated. They could then return and possess the land. The Jews encouraged the Arabs to stay.

The hated "Jewish Zionists" did not force the Arab Palestinians to leave. Their own leaders forced them to leave the land. This created the Palestinian refugee problem. The Arab countries have refused to assimilate the Palestinians and care for their needs. Instead, they continue to use them as political pawns in their struggle against Israel.

Promising them glory, money, and paradise with 72 beautiful virgins, the PLO and other terrorist organizations have no problem recruiting young Palestinians to fight the "Zionists" enemy. These terrorist organizations are well financed by the "moderate" Saudi Arabian rulers, as well and Syria and Iran. They have all the money they need for weapons, and are very skillful at manipulating the Western media to brainwash the American public to believe their propaganda. Only God knows how the American defeat of Saddam Hussein will change the Middle East and terrorism.

The United Nations Relief and Works Agency, (UNRWA) was given the responsibility of administering the refugee problem. The money given by the UNRWA to assist the "refugees" comes primarily from the American taxpayer. This is a big business with thousands profiting from it. With so much money involved, there is little interest in ending the plight of the displaced Palestinians. The real legitimate right of the Palestinians is to be assimilated by the Arab countries from which they initially came.

The God of the Bible loves the Arab people, but He has a different plan for them than He does for the Jews. God will bless the Arabs if they will submit to His plans and purposes. He will judge them if they do not. We will have continued conflict until the Almighty Himself brings it to an end.

In His own time, God will end this conflict by giving Israel a great victory. This will show the nations of the world and the Arab people that the God of Abraham, Isaac, and Jacob is the one true God. The prophet Zechariah tells us:

> *In that day the Lord will defend the inhabitants of Jerusalem; the one who is feeble among them in that day shall be like David, and the house of David shall be like God, like the*

Angel of the Lord before them. It shall be in that day that I will seek to destroy all the nations that come against Jerusalem.[14]

Israel's victory will cause a great spiritual awakening within the Islamic nations. Many will turn to the one true God of Israel as the prophet Isaiah predicted.

In that day Israel will be one of three with Egypt and Assyria—a blessing in the midst of the land, who the Lord of hosts shall bless, saying, "Blessed is Egypt My people, and Assyria the work of My hand, and Israel My inheritance."[15]

Israel's victory will also cause many Jewish people to return to their biblical heritage and seek the God of their ancestors as Joel explains: "So you shall know that I am the Lord your God, dwelling in Zion My holy mountain. Then Jerusalem shall be holy, and no aliens shall ever pass through her again."[16]

The prophet Ezekiel adds the following:

"I will set My glory among the nations; all the nations shall see My judgment which I have executed, and My hand which I have laid on them. So the house of Israel shall know that I am the Lord their God from that day forward....And I will not hide My face from them anymore; for I shall have poured out My Spirit on the house of Israel," says the Lord God.[17]

Furthermore, the nations of the world will realize there is a God in Heaven active in world affairs and is moving forward the course of human history according to His own plans and purposes for mankind. He is the God of the Bible, the God of Abraham, Isaac, and Jacob.

Once again, the Lord speaks through the prophet Ezekiel, "Thus I will magnify Myself and sanctify Myself, and I will be known in the eyes of many nations. Then they shall know that I am the Lord."[18]

Until the time when the Almighty brings an end to the Middle East conflict, Christians and Jews must pray and actively seek the peace of Jerusalem (Psalm 122:6) and stand together against radical Islam that would destroy Israel and dominate the Christian world.

Personal Study Review

1. Explain the family feud between the line of Ishmael and the line of Isaac.
2. Explain the Muslim concept of the "House of Peace" and the "House of War."
3. Who are the Palestinians?
4. How and why will this conflict end?

Chapter 6

MIDDLE EAST MYTHS PART 1

An excited crowd of 5,000 Christian Zionists attending the Feast of Tabernacles in Jerusalem leaped to their feet with thunderous applause when then Prime Minister Benjamin Netanyahu asked them to join Israel in their historic struggle to present the true story of Israel and the Arab world. Israel has certainly been losing the battle for truth to Arab propaganda that is expert in turning Arab fantasies into facts and Israeli facts into fantasies.

A once proud Israel, weakened by Arab propaganda and internal dissension and, in desperate longings for peace, is willing to appease their enemies to their own detriment. Britain followed the same policy of trying to bring peace to the Middle East by appeasing intimidation and terror. From the wisdom of someone who knows, Winston Churchill would caution us that "acts of appeasement today will have to be remedied at far greater cost and remorse tomorrow."[1]

A strong, secure Israel is in the national interest of the United States politically, militarily, economically, socially, and spiritually. It is important politically as Israel is the only democratic state in the Middle East. It is important militarily as a front line defense against radical Islamic fundamentalism. It is important economically because a strong Israel deters Arab aggression which stabilizes oil prices. It is important socially as it shares our values of freedom and the sanctity of human life. It is important spiritually in regard to Judeo-Christian ethics that serve as the foundation of Western culture.

If Israel succumbs to radical, Islamic fundamentalism, American Judeo-Christian culture, synagogues and churches will be threatened. Today, it's Joseph's tomb that is desecrated. Tomorrow, it's our synagogues and churches.

American citizens, both Jews and Christians, need to enlist as soldiers in the battle for truth regarding the Arab-Israeli conflict. This conflict is spiritual in nature, and the final outcome is clear. The God of the Bible made an everlasting covenant with the Jewish people, and He is a faithful covenant-keeping God (Genesis 17). Yet, a famous passage in the Bible says to "pray for [actively seek the peace of] Jerusalem."[2]

Christian and Jewish supporters of Israel are not anti-Arab. The battle for truth is not against the Arab people. God loves all people the same, but He has different plans and purposes for different people groups. The root cause of the conflict in the Middle East is due to the fact that radical Islamic Arab leaders are seeking to establish and extend themselves beyond the limits God has set for them and in opposition to the One True God.

THE BOOK AND THE LAND

David Ben-Gurion expressed the motivation and expectation for joining this battle for truth in his statement on November 29,

1947, regarding the United Nations partition of Palestine. He said, "I know that God promised all of Palestine to the children of Israel. I do not know what borders He set. I believe they are wider than the ones proposed. If God will keep His promise in His own time, our business as poor humans who live in a difficult age is to save as much as we can of the remnants of Israel."[3]

British military officer Captain Orde Wingate played an important role in the establishment of the state of Israel. When asked by his Jewish friends why he supported them, he said, "There is only one important book on the subject, the Bible, and I have read it thoroughly. This is the cause of your survival. I count it as my privilege to help you fight your battle. To that purpose I want to devote my life...I shall fight with you against any of these influences. But remember that it is your battle. My part, which I say I feel to be a privilege, is only to help you."[4]

As "People of the Book," Jews and Christians must look to the Bible as the standard of truth regarding this conflict. And the Bible clearly promises the land to the Jewish people with Jerusalem as their eternal and undivided capital. If one reads the Bible for the plain sense of its meaning, there is no way to misunderstand what it says. We can be confident that the God of Abraham, Isaac, and Jacob will keep His promise in His own time and way to save the remnant of Israel. Until then, Jews and Christians must work together in the battle for truth.

Middle East Myths

Joseph Goebbels, Nazi Minister of Propaganda and Information, said that a big lie that is told often enough and long enough will eventually be accepted as truth. With cooperation from the world's media, coupled with ignorance, apathy, and anti-Semitism among the nations, Israel is being presented as a giant Goliath killing little Davids who are only armed with stones.

We are told there would be peace in the Middle East if only Goliath Israel would agree to little David's demand for a Palestinian state with Jerusalem as its capital. This is one of the many lies constantly repeated to the uninformed West. The purpose of Chapter Six and Chapter Seven is to expose some of the myths regarding the Arab-Israeli conflict.

MYTH #1 - THE MYTH OF PALESTINE

In an article entitled, "The Lesson of Palestine," printed in the *Middle East Journal*, October 1949, Arab activist, Musa Alami, wrote, "How can people struggle for their nation, when most of them do not know the meaning of the word?...The people are in great need of a 'myth' of imagination. The myth of nationality would create 'identity' and 'self-respect.'"[5]

The Arab world has certainly demonstrated great skill in the "myth" of imagination. They have done such a good job that they have convinced much of the world that their "myths" are facts. Perhaps their biggest myth is the myth of Palestine. The Arab world would have us believe that the Palestinians have been in "Palestine" from "time immemorial" but were displaced by the Jews when Israel became a state in 1948. But what are the facts?

While we are not certain of the exact dates, Joshua conquered the Land God promised the Jews in the 13th century B.C.E. King David established Jerusalem as the capital of Israel around 1000 B.C.E. King Solomon built the Jewish Temple about 960 B.C.E. This was almost 1,000 years before the beginning of Christianity and 1,600 years before the rise of Islam.

As Prime Minister Barak has noted, "When Jesus came to Jerusalem to celebrate the feasts, he didn't come to a church or a mosque, he came to the Temple." It is not the Church Mount or the Mosque Mount that is fought over, it is the Temple Mount. It was the Temple Mount centuries before Christianity tried to make it the Church Mount and Islam tried to make it the Mosque Mount.

However, not to be confused with facts, in a personal audience I had several years ago with the Grand Mufti of Jerusalem, who was appointed by Arafat, he boldly declared that the Arabs had been living in the Land for 10,000 years. Based on conservative Bible chronology, that means the Arabs have been living in the Land before the Almighty created Adam and Eve.

How did Israel become Palestine and who are the Palestinians? The second Jewish war with the Romans took place in A.D. 132-135. Led by Rabbi Akiva and Simon bar Kochba, the Jewish uprising was crushed by the Roman Emperor Hadrian who sought to de-Judaize Jerusalem and make it a pagan city. Hadrian renamed Jerusalem "Aelia Capitolina" in honor of Jupiter. He changed the name of Judea and gave it the name of the Jews ancient enemy, the Philistines. As we learned in the last chapter, Hadrian called the land–Palestine.

Over time, Palestine was ruled by the Roman Byzantines (312-637) [Persian interrupt 614-629], Omayyad Arabs (638-750), Islamic Abbassid's (750-1099), Crusaders (1099-1291) [Saladin the Kurd interrupt 1187-93], Mamluks (1291-1516), Ottoman Turks (1517-1917), and the British Mandate (1917-1948).

None of these rulers ever established a sovereign state in the land and Jerusalem was never the capital of any empire since the time of King David. Palestine was a forgotten desolate, wasteland, but historical records show there was always a Jewish presence in the land.

The revival of modern Jewish life in the land began in the 1880s with the arrival of Russian refugees from the Russian pogroms. A second wave of immigration, also from Russia, was in 1905. This was followed by later immigrations resulting in a growing Jewish population in the land.

When the Jews came to the Land, they found a malaria infested swamp in the north and an uninhabitable desert in the south. It was as if the God of the Bible had kept the land hidden away in obscurity until the rightful owners—the Jews returned to claim it.

The Jewish pioneers did not steal the Land from the Arabs. They purchased the land at highly inflated prices from absentee landlords living outside the land. As the Jews worked the land, it began to prosper.

While there were Jews and Arabs living in the land, there were many poor migrant Arab farm workers in the surrounding Arab countries who needed work. When they heard that the land was prospering under the hand of the Jews, they migrated to Palestine to get work from the Jews. Furthermore, the British allowed many thousands of Arabs into Palestine illegally while barring the Jews from entering the land. For the most part, the Arab Palestinians are these peasant farm workers and illegal aliens.

"Palestinians" have never been a distinct people, they have never had a sovereign land called Palestine, Jerusalem has never been their capital, there is no Palestinian language or culture, and there is no such group as a Palestinian people. It is a myth created after the Jews liberated Jerusalem in 1967.

Before the birth of the State of Israel, Arab leaders themselves denied the existence of an Arab country called Palestine. In 1937, Arab leader, Auni Bey Abdul-Hadi said, "There is no such country [as Palestine]! 'Palestine' is a term the Zionists invented! There is no Palestine in the Bible. 'Palestine" is alien to us; it is the Zionists who introduced it."[6]

In 1946, a distinguished Princeton professor and Arab historian said, "There is no such thing as Palestine in Arab history, absolutely not."[7]

All who lived in the land, Jews, Arabs, and Christians, were called Palestinians. In fact, the Jerusalem Post was called the Palestinian Post. Under the British Mandate, the Palestinian Jews were given a state. But before this state came into existence, Colonial Secretary, Winston Churchill, in 1922, took away 77 percent of the geographic area promised to the Jews and created *Tran-Jordan* as a state for the Palestinian Arabs. Israel would be for the Palestinian Jews and Transjordan (now Jordan) for the Palestinian Arabs.

Israel became a state in the War of Independence in 1948. At that time, approximately 600,000 Arabs fled to become refugee pawns in the hands of neighboring Arab states. Some number of Arabs stayed to become Israeli citizens. While we certainly sympathize with the plight of the Arab refugees, their problems could easily be solved if their Arab brothers cared enough to assimilate them as the Jews did their own 800,000 immigrants from the Arab countries.

Myth #2 - The Myth of Al Quds

In the Bible, the prophet Zechariah writes of the time when God will gather all the nations to battle against Jerusalem.

> *Behold, I will make Jerusalem a cup of drunkenness to all the surrounding peoples, when they lay siege against Judah and Jerusalem. And it shall happen in that day that I will make Jerusalem a very heavy stone for all peoples; all who would heave it away will surely be cut in pieces, though all nations of the earth are gathered against it.*[8]
>
> *It shall be in that day that I will seek to destroy all the nations that come against Jerusalem.*[9]

We are seeing this battle unfold before our very eyes with Israel and the Arabs on the front lines of the battle. But according to the Bible and unfolding events, the nations will also soon join in the battle. For the purpose of this discussion, we want to look at the battle in view of the historical claims Islam has on the Temple Mount as the "third holiest sight" in Islam. The Arab word used for Jerusalem, which you hear often in the media, is "Al Quds." Let's consider the "Myth of Al Quds."

JERUSALEM IN THE BIBLE AND THE KORAN

You can tell how important a person, place or thing is to people by how often they speak of that person, place or place. We speak most about what we love and cherish. Since people talk about that which is most dear to them, we should be able to get a good idea of how important Jerusalem is to Jews and Arabs by reading their holy books, the Bible for the Jews and the Koran for the Arab Muslims.

We discover that Jerusalem is mentioned over 800 times in the Bible. There are 657 references in the Tanakh (Hebrew Bible) and 154 references in the New Testament. Yet, Jerusalem is not mentioned even once in the Koran. And there is no reason that it should be because Mohammed never went to Jerusalem. In Mohammed's lifetime, Jerusalem was outside the sphere of Islam.

This should make it clear that historically, Jerusalem is very important to the Jews, but has had little or no importance to Muslims until recent times. Furthermore, observant Jews pray facing Jerusalem while Muslims pray facing Mecca. Jews make pilgrimages to Jerusalem and Muslims make pilgrimages to Mecca.

The Temple Mount became part of Islam long after the time of Mohammed. And this was for political reasons arising out of the military expansion of Islam. It was certainly not for religious purposes. And even then, Muslims have only seemed to be interested in Jerusalem and the Temple Mount when the Jews control them. So how is it that the Temple Mount has become the "third holiest site of Islam?

Mohammed's Night Flight

The Koran states, "Glory be to him who made His servant [Mohammed] go by night from the Sacred Mosque to the farthest [or remotest] Mosque."[10] All agree that the Sacred Mosque is in Mecca. It's the location of the farthest or remotest Mosque that has been unclear.

Earliest views were that the farthest mosque referred to Medina. It wasn't until the seventh century that some Islamic leaders identified it with Jerusalem. The legend is that Mohammed, either literally, or in a dream/vision made a journey to heaven from Mecca with a stopover in Jerusalem.

Mohammed's second wife, Ayesha, said that on the night Mohammed was supposed to make this night flight, he was sleeping soundly by her side.[11] In view of her testimony, Mohammed's night flight has often been presented as a dream or vision rather than as a literal event, although there are still those who choose not to be confused with facts and present Mohammed's flight as a literal happening.

The story is that Mohammed flew north on his horse, Burak, which had two wings and the face of a human. After stops at Mt. Sinai and Bethlehem, they landed at the sight of the mosque in Jerusalem.

At this point, heaven lowered a ladder to carry Mohammed to the Seventh Heaven where he was met by Abraham, Isaac, Joseph, Moses, and Jesus and received their blessing to become the last prophet of God. Mohammed then returned by the ladder to Jerusalem from whence Burak flew him back to Mecca. Moslems point to the footprint Burak left when Mohammed leaped onto his back for the return trip to Mecca.

Now all religions, including my own, have their legends. I am certainly not the one to judge them. But the problem with this one is that Mohammed died decades before a mosque was built on the Temple Mount. So Jerusalem and the Temple Mount cannot possibly be the location of the farthest mosque mentioned in the Koran.

Mohammed died in 632, six years before Jerusalem fell to the Arabs under Caliph Omar in 638. The Dome of the Rock was not built until 692, which was 60 years after Mohammed's death. The Al-Aqsa Mosque was not built until 712, which is 80 years after Mohammed's death.

THE MOSQUE ON THE TEMPLE MOUNT

The Caliph Omar defeated the Byzantine Christians in 636 at the battle of the Yarmuk River. Jerusalem surrendered to him in 638. Until this time, Jerusalem had been outside the realm of Islam. Caliph Omar built a small house of prayer near the rock on the site of the destroyed Jewish Temple. The purpose was to show that Islam had replaced Judaism and Christianity as the last divine revelation.

Later, the Umayyad Caliph Abd al-Malik, whose capital was in Damascus, built the Dome of the Rock on the same site. Twenty years later, his son, Caliph al-Walid built the Al-Aqsa Mosque. Aqsa is Arabic for furthermost or remotest. As a way of establishing a legitimate claim of Islam over the Temple Mount, this mosque has been identified as the one spoken of in the Koran.

Historians tell us that Abd al-Malik built the Dome of the Rock on the site to: (1) link himself as the successor to King Solomon, (2) to contradict Jesus' statement that the Temple would be destroyed (Matthew 24, Luke 21), (3) To compete against spectacular church sites such as the Church of the Holy Sepulcher, and (4) to encourage Muslim worshipers in his territory to make pilgrimages to the Dome of the Rock rather than making pilgrimages outside of his territory to his rival Caliph in Mecca.[12]

Abd al-Malik was eager to emphasize the independence and the triumph of the new religion over Christianity both militarily and ideologically. He put a lengthy Arabic inscription on the Dome of the Rock condemning Christianity. It contains many verses from the Koran, but not the one about Mohammed's night journey. Surely, he would have included that verse if he thought it referred to the Temple Mount Mosque.

While Abd al-Malik considered building the Dome of the Rock on top of the place where Solomon's Temple stood, Islamic leaders today deny there was even a Jewish Temple on the Mount.

Mohammed and the Jews

As pointed out in Chapter Four, Mohammed held the Jews in high esteem and even tried to befriend them. Oddly enough, he recognized that the Jews were God's chosen people and that God had promised them the Land. Recall the following quotations from the Koran which are certainly not politically correct statements today.

"O Children of Israel! Remember…that I exalted you above all people"[13]

"Remember, my people, the favor which Allah bestowed upon you. He has raised up prophets among you, made you kings, and given you that which he has given to no other nation [the land]. Enter my people, the holy land which Allah has assigned for you."[14]

Remember that when Mohammed was forced to flee Mecca, he went to Yathrib, later renamed Medina. I explained in Chapter Four that Yathrib was founded by Jews and populated by Jews as well as Arabs. Remember that Mohammed sought to win over the Jews to his new religion by declaring Muslims should face Jerusalem when they pray. But when the Jews refused to acknowledge Mohammed as a prophet, he turned against them and slaughtered all he could. He then literally did an about face and declared Muslims should face Mecca to pray. He then slaughtered the Jews and eventually proclaimed that Islam would be the only religion of Arabia. Arabs and Jews have been in conflict ever since.

In spite of Arab propaganda to the contrary, the Temple Mount is not sacred to Islam. The Temple Mount is the focus of Islam only when it is not under Muslim control. Jordan controlled East Jerusalem and the Temple Mount from 1948-1967. During that time, no Arab leader thought it important to make Jerusalem an Arab capital and no significant leader from the Arab world thought it necessary to come to pray at the Mosque. It was only in 1967, when the Jews liberated the Temple Mount from Arab control that it became the "third holiest site in Islam."

As the battle for truth rages, the God of Israel will soon reveal the truth concerning these issues. He will return to Zion at which time Jerusalem will be called the "City of Truth." The prophet Zechariah explains, "Thus says the Lord: 'I will return to Zion and dwell in the midst of Jerusalem. Jerusalem shall be called the City of Truth, the mountain of the Lord of hosts, the Holy Mountain.'"[15]

Personal Study Review

1. Explain the myth of Palestine.
2. Explain the myth of Al Quds.
3. Explain Mohammed's night flight and how it relates to the Muslim claim to the Temple Mount.
4. The Muslim religious leaders who control the Temple Mount have hauled away large truckloads of dirt and rock from the Temple Mount and discarded this in trash piles outside the walls of the Old City. Why do you think they have done this?

Chapter 7

Middle East Myths Part 2

Where would we be without Webster's dictionary? Our old scholar and friend, Mr. Webster defines a myth as a person or thing existing only in imagination. *Myths*, Webster tells us, are arbitrary, fictitious inventions. In other words, they are "made up" by people for their own purposes. Some people are real experts when it comes to inventing myths. They have an abnormal propensity for lying and exaggerating. They can be so skilled at mythmaking that they believe their own myths.

Let me give you an example. A certain man was resting in his hammock when his neighbor came by and told him there was a big sale on figs and dates at the market. There was no sale at the market. The neighbor just wanted to rest in the hammock. Yet, he was so convincing, his slumbering acquaintance got out of the hammock and went to the "big sale" at the market. The neighbor then took a nap in the hammock.

The neighbor, who was now in the hammock, had barely been resting long enough to close his eyes when he decided that the big sale at the market was too much for him to miss. Believing his own myth, he got out of the hammock and went to the market to take advantage of the sale.

The Arab propaganda machine is great at turning Israeli facts into myths and Arab myths into facts. They have convinced most of the world that there is a big sale at the market (Jews stole Arab land) and that they, the Arabs, should be sleeping in the hammock (taking back what belongs to them).

Even some who are the victims of the big lie begin to believe it. They hear the big lie so often and presented so convincingly by the mythmaker that, over time, they also come to believe it. Since everyone is repeating the myth it must be true. In this chapter, we continue to study Middle East Myths as we seek truth regarding the Arab-Israeli conflict.

MYTH #3 – THE MYTH THAT JEWS STOLE ARAB LAND

Probably the most repeated and believed myth is that the Jews stole Arab land. But what are the facts? The facts are readily available for anyone wanting to do their own research. Unfortunately, the average person does not have the time or motivation toward self-discovery. Therefore, they are easily deceived by bias news.

Two of the best sources for anyone wanting to do their own research are *From Time Immemorial: The Origins of the Arab-Jewish Conflict Over Palestine* by Joan Peters and *Myths and Facts: A Guide to the Arab-Israeli Conflict* published by American-Israeli Cooperative Enterprise (AICE). The following information regarding ownership of the land at the beginning of World War I is taken from *Myths and Facts*.

"Despite the growth in their population, the Arabs continued to assert they were being displaced. The truth is from the beginning of World War I, part of Palestine's land was owned by absentee landlords who lived in Cairo, Damascus and Beirut. About 80 percent of the Palestinian Arabs were debt-ridden peasants, semi-nomads and Bedouins.

"Jews actually went out of their way to avoid purchasing land in areas where Arabs might be displaced. They sought land that was largely uncultivated, swampy, cheap and, most important, without tenants.

"In 1920, David Ben-Gurion expressed his concern about the Arab *fellahin*, whom he viewed as 'the most important asset of the native population.' Ben-Gurion said, 'Under no circumstances must we touch land belonging to the *fellahs* or worked by them.' He advocated helping liberating them from their oppressors. 'Only if a fellah leaves his place of settlement,' Ben-Gurion added, 'should we offer to buy his land, at an appropriate price.'

"It was only after the Jews had bought all of this available land that they began to purchase cultivated land. Many Arabs were willing to sell because of the migration to coastal towns and because they needed money to invest in the citrus industry.

"When John Hope Simpson arrived in Palestine in May 1930, he observed: 'They [Jews] paid high prices for the land, and in addition they paid to certain of the occupants of those lands a considerable amount of money which they were not legally bound to pay.'

"In 1931, Lewis French conducted a survey of landlessness and eventually offered new plots to any Arabs who had been 'dispossessed.' British officials received more than 3,000 applicants, of which 80 percent were ruled invalid by the Government's legal advisor because the applicants were not landless Arabs. This left only about 600 landless Arabs, 100 of whom accepted the Government land offer.

"In November, 1936, the British Peel Commission reported that Arab complaints about Jewish land acquisition were baseless. It pointed out that 'much of the land now carrying orange groves was sand dunes or swamp and uncultivated when it was purchased....there was at the time of the earlier sales little evidence that the owners possessed either the recourses or training needed to develop the land.'

"Moreover, the Commission found the shortage was 'due less to the amount of land acquired by Jews than to the increase in the Arab population.' The report concluded that the presence of Jews in Palestine, along with the work of the British Administration, had resulted in higher wages, an improved standard of living and ample employment opportunities.

"Even at the height of the Arab revolt in 1938, the British High Commissioner to Palestine believed the Arab landowners were complaining about sales to Jews to drive up prices for lands they wished to sell. Many Arab landowners had been so terrorized by Arab rebels they decided to leave Palestine and sell their property to the Jews. The Jews were paying exorbitant prices to wealthy landowners for small tracts of arid land. 'In 1944, Jews paid between $1,000 and $1,100 per acre in Palestine for arid or semiarid land; in the same year, rich black soil in Iowa was selling for about $110 per acre.'

"By 1947, Jewish holdings in Palestine amounted to about 463,000 acres. Approximately 45,000 of these acres were acquired from the Mandatory government; 30,000 were bought from various churches and 387,500 were purchased from Arabs. Analyses of land purchases from 1880 to 1948 show that 73 percent of Jewish plots were purchased from large landowners, not poor *fellahin*. Many prominent Arab leaders sold land to the Jews."[1]

Myth #4 - The Myth of Arab Refugees

When Israel became a nation, 800,000 Jewish refugees fled from the Arab states to Israel. While it took tremendous sacrifice on the part of the new nation, these refugees, whose land and money was confiscated by the Arabs, were assimilated in the fledgling new state and became productive citizens of Israel. The growing Arab Palestinian population was not as fortunate.

Arab leaders from the neighboring countries declared war against Israel. They then instructed the Arab Palestinians to flee the Jewish state until the Jews were annihilated. They then could return and possess the land. While there is no doubt that Jewish fighters drove some Arabs away, the Jewish leaders encouraged the Arabs to stay. The great majority of Arabs were not expelled but left without ever seeing an Israeli soldier.

Myths and Facts gives the following information:

"The Palestinians left their homes in 1947-1948 for a variety of reasons. Thousands of wealthy Arabs left in anticipation of a war, thousands more responded to Arab leaders' calls to get out of the way of the advancing armies, a handful were expelled, but most simply fled to avoid being caught in the cross fire of a battle.

"Many Arabs claim that 800,000 to 1,000,000 Palestinians became refugees in 1947-1949. The last census was taken by the British in 1945. It found approximately 1.2 million permanent Arab residents in all of Palestine. On November 30, 1947, the date the UN voted for partition, the total within the boundaries of the State of Israel was 809,100. A 1949 Government of Israel census reported 160,000 Arabs living in the country after the war. This meant no more than 650,000 Palestinian Arabs could have become refugees. A report by the UN Mediator on Palestine arrived at even lower figure—472,000.

"Although much is heard about the plight of the Palestinian refugees, little is said about the Jews who fled from Arab states. Their situation had long been precarious. During the 1947 UN debates, Arab leaders threatened them. For example, Egypt's delegate told the General Assembly: 'the lives of one million Jews in Muslim countries would be jeopardized by partition.'

"The number of Jews fleeing Arab countries for Israel in the years following Israel's independence was roughly equal to the number of Arabs leaving Palestine. Many Jews were allowed to take little more than the shirts on their backs. These refugees had no desire to be repatriated. Little is heard about them because they did not remain refugees for long. Of the 820,000 Jewish refugees, 586,000 were resettled in Israel at great expense, and without any offer of compensation from the Arab governments who confiscated their possessions.

> Israel has consequently maintained that any agreement to compensate the Palestinian refugees must also include Arab compensation for Jewish refugees. To this day, the Arab states have refused to pay any compensation to the hundreds of thousands of Jews who were forced to abandon their property before fleeing those countries[2] (page 162).

We see that the hated "Jewish-Zionists" did not force the Arab Palestinians to leave. Their own leaders forced them to leave the land or they left of their own accord. They were responsible for causing their own Arab Palestinian refugee problem. The Arab countries, with all their great wealth, resources, and land have refused to assimilate the Arab Palestinians and care for their needs. Instead, they continue to use them as political pawns in their struggle against Israel.

Promising them glory, money, and paradise, and I might add CNN cameras, the PLO and other terrorist organizations have no problem recruiting young Arab Palestinians to fight the "Zionist" enemy. In fact, Yasser Arafat conducted youth camps where he taught young people how to fight the Jews. Now that he has died, those who have taken his place continue the camps. They dress up small children in uniforms and teach them how to blow themselves up as martyrs. And as the whole world now knows, they send children out to fight their battles for them.

MYTH #5 - THE MYTH OF MOSLEM TOLERANCE

Another myth is that that Jews who lived under Muslim Arab rule before the birth of Israel had harmonious relations with the Arabs and were treated with dignity and tolerance. The implication is that if Israel would submit to Arab rule, the fighting would stop and Muslims, Jews, and Christians in the Middle East would live happily ever after. But what are the facts?

Prior to the time of Mohammed, Jews and Arabs did live in relative peace with one another. However, as we learned in previous chapters, when the Jews rejected Mohammed as a prophet, he turned against them with a vengeance as seen in his violent actions against the Jews. His negative attitude is found in the many hostile comments against Jews in the Koran and the Hadith.

The caliph who succeeded Mohammed was Omar. He produced a document called the *Omar Charter* in which he codified the conditions Jews were to live by under Islamic Arab rule. Here are some of the conditions of peace and fraternity the Jews enjoyed. Christians lived under similar restrictions.

1. Jews were forbidden to touch the Koran.
2. Jews were required to wear distinctive clothing.
3. Jews were required to wear a yellow piece of cloth as a badge (blue for Christians).

4. Jews were not allowed to perform their religious practices in public.
5. Jews were not allowed to own a horse which was a sign of a nobleman.
6. Jews were required to bury their dead without grieving in public.
7. Jews were required to pay special taxes.
8. Jews were not allowed to defend themselves against a Moslem.
9. Jews were not allowed to testify against a Moslem.
10. Jews were forbidden to build new synagogues.
11. The houses and tombs of Jews were not allowed to be higher than those of the Moslems.
12. The graves of Jews had to be level so that anyone could walk over them.[3]

Throughout the centuries, Jews and Christians living under Islamic rule suffered great persecution and humiliation, the intensity of which was determined by the character of the particular Moslem ruler. With few exceptions, Jews and Christians struggled to survive and lived in constant fear for their lives.

In more modern times, when Jordan illegally occupied East Jerusalem from 1948-1967, all Jewish residents were expelled and forbidden to worship at the Western Wall. The Jewish quarter, including all 58 synagogues, was destroyed or desecrated. Approximately 75 percent of the tombstones on the Jewish cemetery on the Mount of Olives were dismantled and used as part of the Jordanian army latrines. This was done under the rule of King Hussein, the most moderate of the Arab rulers and we see what he allowed under his rule.[4]

Life was not much better for Christians living under Moslem rule. Christians were forbidden to ring their church bells. The ban lasted for 1,000 years until the middle of the 19th century. While church bells were silent, the muezzin called out five times a day, "There is no god but Allah and Mohammad is his prophet."[5]

There is no doubt that an Islamic Palestinian state would turn synagogues and churches into mosques and expel Jews and Christians or force them into a life of fear and humiliation. Does the Christian world really want Hamas to control the Church of the Holy Sepulcher, the empty tomb and Manger Square? Does the Jewish world really want Hamas to control the Temple Mount, the Mount of Olives and the Old City? Do Jews and Christians in Israel and in America really want to live under Islamic rule? Do we care or are we too comfortable to be bothered?

MYTH #6 - THE MYTH OF YASSER ARAFAT

One of the greatest myths is the myth of Yasser Arafat. To understand the deception of Yasser Arafat, we must look briefly at the situation in pre-Israel Palestine during the British Mandate. The moral of this story is that those who do not know history are doomed to repeat it.

At the end of the First World War, Britain was given the mandate to administer Palestine. At that time, the British government appointed Sir Herbert Samuel, a British Jew, as Palestine High Commissioner. Sir Herbert Samuel arrived in Palestine on July 1, 1920. Unfortunately, history tells us that Sir Herbert was a weak administrator who was eager to compromise for what he thought would bring peace.[6]

Perhaps because he was a Jew, and not wanting to appear partial, Sir Herbert appeased the extremist, nationalistic Arab minority led by a violent, fanatical zealot named Haj Amin al-Husseini.

Husseini was from a prominent Arab Palestinian family who were fervent Anti-Zionists. The British had earlier imprisoned Husseini for instigating an Arab attack against Jews who were praying at the Western Wall.[7]

A crisis that would have lasting consequences occurred in 1921 when the existing Arab Mufti (religious leader) died. Due to influence by anti-Zionist British officials on his staff, Sir Herbert released Husseini from prison and appointed him as the new Mufti, even elevating him to the title of Grand Mufti. He became the religious and political leader of the Arabs. Husseini was only in his mid-twenties at this time, but he already had a history of violence against Jews.[8]

Husseini was the first proponent of militant, Arab Palestinian nationalism. He was an all or nothing terrorist who was determined to drive out or destroy the Jews or be destroyed himself, regardless of how many lives were wasted in the process. Once he was in power, he began a campaign of terror and intimidation against anyone opposed to his rule and policies. He not only killed Jews but also Arabs who did not support his campaign of violence. Husseini was not willing to negotiate or make any kind of compromise for the sake of peace.[9]

Once again we turn to Winston Churchill who tried to reason with the Arabs with the Western understanding of "give and take" so that all parties would have at least some of their demands satisfied. Churchill tried to explain the Arab mind to his Western colleagues. He would tell how the Arabs refused to negotiate but came to the "peace talks" thinking they could give nothing while expecting the other side to make huge concessions with no guarantees that the concessions would lead to peace. What baffled Churchill was that the Arabs were unwilling to offer even the smallest percent in order to get practically everything they wanted. They had no consideration of the claims and needs of others, but only their own.

Many moderate Arabs fled Palestine out of fear of Husseini. He raised the stakes of the Arab-Jewish conflict and took control away from the more moderate Arabs who desired to live in peace with the Jews. Mainly because of him, attempts to establish peaceful relations between Arabs and Jews came to an end. He plunged the Arab world into a political and religious "jihad" against the Jewish people that set the course for the Arab-Israeli conflict in the Middle East.[10]

Husseini instigated bloody riots against the Jews in 1920-1921 and again in 1929. In 1929, Husseini concocted a story that the Jews praying at the Western Wall were taking over the Al-Aqsua Mosque. Sound familiar? He massacred the Jews at the Wall. This triggered a riot by Arabs in Hebron. On the Sabbath of August 24, Arabs murdered 67 Jewish men, women and children in Hebron and destroyed the synagogues. This violent action brought an end to a Jewish presence in Hebron that had been there for thousands of years.[11]

He saw Hitler's "final solution to the Jewish problem" as the answer to his own desire to eliminate the presence of Jews in Palestine. Husseini imported Nazi influence into Palestine and used Nazi funds to finance his terrorist activities. He openly supported Hitler and Mussolini and led a revolt against the British in 1936-1939. He was forced to flee to Iraq where he cooperated with the Nazis in a failed coup attempt against the British. He then fled to Germany where, in November of 1941, he was greeted with open arms by Hitler himself.[12]

Husseini was known as the "Arab Fuehrer." He used his program on *Radio Berlin* to exhort the Arabs in the Middle East to murder the Jews in a holy war that pleased Allah. While at the same time, he prodded the Nazis to further zeal in completing their "final solution to the Jewish problem." In one instance, he learned that Adolf Eichman intended to swap thousands of Jewish children for German POWs. His protest forced Eichman to cancel the swap, resulting in the children being sent to death camps in Poland.[13]

On another occasion, Husseini traveled to Bosnia where he recruited Bosnian Moslems for the SS. They slaughtered ninety percent of Bosnia's Jews. The only condition Husseini set for assisting the Nazis was that, after they won the war, they would murder all the Jews in Palestine. After the war was over, Husseini fled to Cairo where he was given a heroes welcome.[14]

During the war, Arab Nazi parties were founded throughout the Middle East. The most influential one was "Young Egypt" which was established in 1933. Young Egypt imitated the Nazi party in their ideology, slogans, processionals, and anti-Semitic actions. When the war was over, a member of Young Egypt named Gamal Abdul Nasser led the coup in 1952 that overthrew the Egyptian government. He made Egypt a safe haven for Nazi war criminals and, in 1964, he established the Palestinian Liberation Organization (PLO).[15]

Eventually the leadership of the PLO was taken over by a man named Rahman Abdul Rauf al-Qudwa al-Husseini. Al-Husseini was a nephew and great admirer of Uncle Haj Amin al-Husseini. He was born in Cairo in 1929 and grew up in the Gaza strip. His mother, Hamida, was a cousin of the Grand Mufti. Due to internal Arab strife, his father Abdul Rauf al-Qudwa was forced to flee Gaza where the family took refuge in Egypt.[16]

Al-Husseini's cousin is Faisal al-Husseini who is the grandson of Haj Amin al-Husseini and the PLO representative in Jerusalem who has directed attacks on the Jews praying at the Western Wall. When Rahman Abdul Rauf al-Qudwa al-Husseini enrolled at the University of Cairo in 1951, he decided to conceal his true identity and registered under the name "Yasser Arafat."[17]

Yes, Uncle Haj, the Arab Fuhrer himself, passed his legacy of hatred of Jews to his nephew Yasser Arafat who has passed the same legacy of hatred to the next generation of young Arabs. Now a whole new generation of Palestinian Arabs has been educated to hate the Jews. Unfortunately, there will be continued violence.

Through the PLO, Arafat sought to further the Arab Nazi goal of eliminating the Jews from the Land. This is why he would never keep any agreement he made with Israel. He did not want to live in peace with Israel. He wanted to destroy Israel. However, like his notorious uncle, Yasser Arafat has failed. He left behind a legacy of hate and destruction and misery for his people. He has passed from the scene and the Israeli flag is still flying high over Jerusalem, the eternal, undivided capital of Israel.

Regardless of the myths regarding the Arab-Israeli conflict, the God of Abraham, Isaac, and Jacob will have the last word on Jerusalem, "Behold, I will save My people for the land of the east and from the land of the west; I will bring them back, and they shall dwell in the midst of Jerusalem. They shall be My people and I will be their God, in truth and righteousness."[18]

Personal Study Review

1. Explain the myth of Jews stealing Arab land.
2. Explain the myth of Arab refugees.
3. Explain the myth of Moslem tolerance.
4. Explain the myth of Yasser Arafat.

Chapter 8

Time to Favor Zion

In spite of how things may appear on the surface, the God of the Bible is Lord over His universe. While He allows man a free will, God will, in His own time and way, put an end to evil and bring peace to the world. Regardless of the sincerity of our world leaders, the "peace process" that is supposed to solve the Arab-Israeli conflict is not working. And it is not going to work because it is contrary to God's will and purposes.

While we appreciate all the hard work by our State Department to bring peace between Israel and her Arab neighbors, the State Department policies have not worked in the past, they are working now and they will not work in the future. Even with the best of intentions, their policies will only bring more war and more suffering.

Former Israeli Prime Minister Rabin used to say, "We don't make peace with our friends but with our enemies." This sounds so nice. Unfortunately, in order to make peace with your enemy, your enemy must want to make peace with you. Israeli's enemies do not want to make peace with Israel. They want to destroy Israel. Israel has no one with whom they can make peace.

God also has a peace process which is different from the peace process of the nations. In fact it is just the opposite. Unfortunately, the nations of the world do not want God's peace process. This is why there is no peace in Jerusalem, the City of Peace.

Whereas the peace process of the nations is to weaken and destroy Israel, God's peace process is to strengthen Israel. The Bible calls God's peace process "Building up Zion." What does this mean? How is the Lord building up Zion? What does this mean for the world? What does this mean for you?

BUILDING UP ZION

One of the most important Bible verses pertaining to our times is found in the book of Psalms. It speaks directly to the Arab-Israeli conflict. It explains God's peace process and reads as follows:

> *But You, O Lord, shall endure forever, and the remembrance of Your name to all generations. You will arise and have mercy on Zion; for the time to favor her, yes, the set time, has come. For your servants take pleasure in her stones, and show favor to her dust. So the nations shall fear the name of the Lord, and all the kings of the earth Your glory. For the Lord shall build up Zion; He shall appear in His glory.*[1]

One of the greatest miracles of our times is the modern rebirth of the nation of Israel. Many people believe this historical event to be a fulfillment of Bible prophecy. Others consider it nothing more than a passing coincidence of world history.

Some favor the rebirth of the nation of Israel while many oppose it. Much of the world's population has probably never given it a thought. They are too busy going about their daily lives to concern themselves with world events. Unaware that God has a sovereign plan for the nations and is actively involved in our world, they have little or no interest.

Yet, we cannot ignore the events taking place in the Middle East. The Arab-Israeli conflict is troubling the whole world and in our news everyday. The headlines of every news media are all about people and countries that seem a world far away, a world about which most of us have never given a thought. But we're thinking about it now.

Jerusalem—A Cup of Trembling

As the Hebrew prophet Zechariah predicted, Jerusalem has become a heavy stone burdening the whole world. Zechariah believed he was speaking for God when he wrote,

> *Behold, I will make Jerusalem a cup of drunkenness* [trembling] *to all the surrounding peoples, when they lay siege against Judah and Jerusalem. And it shall happen in that day that I will make Jerusalem a very heavy stone for all peoples; all who would heave it away will surely be cut in pieces, though all nations of the earth are gathered against it. It shall be in that day that I will seek to destroy all the nations that come against Jerusalem.*[2]

WOW! These profound words were written by Zechariah about 2,600 years ago. Yet they sound like today's headlines. How could this man, who lived such a long time ago, know that Jerusalem would be the cause of distress for all the nations? How could he see the future? The only reasonable explanation is that the God of the Bible really was speaking through the prophet.

Events taking place in Israel as well as among the nations today are happening because of what the writer of Psalms 102 called, "the time to favor Zion." He said the time to favor Zion has come. What did he mean by this? Why should we care and what should be our response, if any?

GOD'S CONTROVERSY WITH THE NATIONS

The time to favor Zion has caused God to have a great controversy with the nations because the nations do not favor Zion. The nations have their own political agenda which is actually opposed to Zion.

The prophet Isaiah wrote of this great controversy many centuries ago. He said, "For it is the day of the Lord's vengeance, the year of recompense for the cause [controversy] of Zion."[3]

The reason why there is continuing trouble in the Middle East is because of the conflict between the sovereign will of God to favor Zion at this time in history and the will of the nations to oppose God's plans and purposes. You may not like that answer but it is clearly stated in the Bible and has been proven in world history and current events.

In spite of the best efforts of world leaders, this controversy will not go away. Although there will be a temporary peace forced on Israel, the Palestinian Arabs, and the Arab nations, it will not last. This is a spiritual issue, not a political one. God's controversy with the nations will continue until the nations submit their will to the God of the Bible.

Because we are living in the period of world history when the One True God has chosen to favor Zion, this controversy will shake and shape the political, military, and economic policies and destiny of the nations. It will also affect the personal destiny of individuals within the nations for good or bad.

As citizens of this world and "People of the Book," Christians and Jews must understand God's agenda and policies and support them. I have previously stated this does not mean we are anti-Arab. It means we are "pro-God." Of course I mean the God of the Bible, not the god of Koran. God has spoken His will through the pen of the Psalmist and many other places in the Bible.

THE LORD'S PLAN

The Bible tells us that the Lord has a definite plan and purpose for creation. God reveals to us through the pen of Isaiah that He has a counsel or plan. He says His plan is from ancient times, or eternity past. God says He is going to fulfill His plan which He calls His pleasure. Then He tells us His pleasure is to place salvation in Zion for Israel My glory.

> *...For I am God, and there is no other; I am God, and there is none like Me, declaring the end from the beginning, and from ancient times things that are not yet done, saying, My counsel shall stand, and I will do all My pleasure...And I will place salvation in Zion for Israel My glory.*[4]

We happen to be living in the period of world history when God is completing His plan. His time to favor Zion has come. Even though the nations of the world hate it and will fight it to the end, God will have His way.

God's plan is to favor Zion. It doesn't matter that human governments consider this plan of God to be politically incorrect. It is politically correct in the government of God, and this is all that matters. The Bible says that Zion, that is Jerusalem, is God's chosen city. Since He is the God of Abraham, Isaac and Jacob, He has chosen Jerusalem, not Mecca, as the place where He will establish His presence on the earth.

The writer of Psalms explains, "For the Lord has chosen Zion; He has desired it for His dwelling place: This is My resting place forever; Here I will dwell, for I have desired it."[5]

"Blessed be the Lord out of Zion, Who dwells in Jerusalem."[6]

Because this is God's peace plan, He cannot bless the plans of governments that oppose His plan. Once again, we turn to the book of Psalms where the Lord says, "Let all who hate Zion be put to shame and turned back."[7] God will turn back, that is, He will judge the nations that oppose Him in His plan to build up Zion.

God's Honor and His Name

In Chapter Four, I mentioned the importance of names. I pointed out that in ancient times; an important part of a people's lives was their name. Their name represented their character, nature, honor, integrity, and their word. Above all else, it was imperative to have a "good name." A person who did not have a good name, and live up to it, could not be trusted.

Because the Lord is God, His highest motivation is to see that His name, which represents Himself, is honored and revered by mankind. God must honor His word and keep His covenant commitments for the sake of His name. God must fulfill His word so that His great name will be honored. If He is not able to do this, then the God of the Bible (Yahweh) is not the true God. The very integrity of God (the Lord), is at stake regarding Israel and Zion.

The prophet Ezekiel describes a time when a powerful nation to the north of Israel will lead a federation of nations in war against Israel. They will greatly outnumber Israel, but the God of Abraham, Isaac and Jacob, the God of Israel, will give Israel a great victory.

Ezekiel says that the Lord will defeat those who attack Israel for His name sake, "Thus I will magnify Myself and sanctify Myself, and I will be known in the eyes of many nations. Then they shall know that I am the Lord."[8]

"So I will make My holy name known in the midst of My people Israel, and I will not let them profane My holy name anymore. Then the nations shall know that I am the Lord, the Holy One in Israel."[9]

The Lord Reigns

As we observe the conflicts taking place in our world, we can't help but be concerned about the outcome. We all wonder what the future holds for the nations as well as our own lives personally. Do you have these thoughts, as I do?

People of the Book need not be concerned. For the Lord has everything under control. He is going to fulfill His plans. It is already an accomplished reality within the heart and mind of God waiting to be revealed on the earth in His own time. Our responsibility is to make sure that our plans are the same as His.

While the nations reject the rule of God over them and have their own agenda, the One True God is not worried. He will judge them for their arrogance and accomplish His will as the Psalmist tells us:

> *The Lord brings the counsel of the nations to nothing; He makes the plans of the people of no effect. The counsel of the Lord stands forever, the plans of His heart to all generations. Blessed is the nation whose God is the Lord, the people He has chosen as His own inheritance.*[10]

The United Nations and the European Union are anti-Semitic to the core. They would love nothing more than to be rid of Israel once and for all. While I'm sure there are honorable diplomats among them, for the most part, they are constantly plotting ways to weaken Israel. Their agenda is contrary to the will of the One True God. They certainly do not want God directing their affairs. This sounds so much like the situation described in the following Psalm:

> *Why do the nations rage, and the people plot a vain thing? The kings of the earth set themselves, and the rulers take counsel together, against the Lord and against His Anointed, saying, "Let us break their bonds in pieces and cast away their cords from us." He who sits in the heavens shall laugh; the Lord shall hold them in derision. Then He shall speak to them in His wrath, and distress them in His deep displeasure: yet I have set My King on My holy hill of Zion.*[11]

The attacks against Israel by the nations of the world are going to get worse in the days ahead. But the Lord God of Israel will defend His people. He will deliver Israel with a great victory over her enemies. The prophet Joel tells us, "And it shall come to pass that whoever calls on the name of the Lord shall be saved. For in Mount Zion and in Jerusalem there shall be deliverance...."[12]

Joel adds this further word of assurance, "The Lord also will roar from Zion, and utter His voice from Jerusalem; the heavens and earth will shake; but the Lord will be a shelter for His people, and the strength of the children of Israel. So you shall know that I am the Lord your God, dwelling in Zion My holy mountain...."[13]

No United Nations, European Union, super power to the West, fanatical ultra-nationalistic to the North, demonic force, religious system, terrorist, or political party, regardless of their good intentions, will hinder the Almighty from accomplishing His will.

When all is said and done, the One True God will be acknowledged by all the nations of the world. This is God's peace process as we learn, once again, from the Psalmist, "All the ends of the world shall remember and turn to the Lord, and all the families of the nations shall worship before You. For the kingdom is the Lord's, and He rules over the nations."[14]

GOD WILL ARISE

The writer of Psalm 102 tells us that God is going to "arise." The Hebrew word for *arise* means "to accomplish, to make good, to help, to perform, to establish, to strengthen, to succeed." These are all active words. They tell us that God is going to take action that will push forward His peace process to build up Zion.

There are people who believe in a Creator-God, but they believe that after God created the universe, He left us to ourselves. They do not believe that God is active in our world. These people apparently have never read the Bible or, if they have, they don't believe it.

The Bible abounds with accounts of God being actively involved in our world overriding evil and working through the normal course of human history to accomplish His will. Furthermore, if the normal course of human activity is not accomplishing His will, God will directly intervene in our world.

Wouldn't it be interesting if we could go back in time and ask certain people to tell us if they believed God was active in the affairs of mankind? In more modern times, we could interview the millions of people whose lives God has dramatically changed if they believe God involves Himself in our lives today.

The Jewish people have understandably asked, "Where was God during the holocaust?" God answers that question from the Hebrew Scriptures. He clearly stated that even though the nations would hate the Jewish people and try to destroy them, He would always preserve a remnant of His people and bring them back to the land He promised them. God did not put Jews in

Hitler's ovens. Satanic inspired people did this horrible thing. Hitler is dead and the people of Israel live.

The Prophet Jeremiah explains, "'For I am with you,' says the Lord, 'to save you; though I make a full end of all nations where I have scattered you, yet I will not make a complete end of you....'"[15]

Ezekiel adds,

> *Thus says the Lord God: "Although I have cast them far off among the Gentiles, and although I have scattered them among the countries, yet I shall be a little sanctuary for them in the countries where they have gone." Therefore say, "Thus says the Lord God: I will gather you from the peoples, assemble you from the countries where you have been scattered, and I will give you the land of Israel."*[16]

God was not the author of the holocaust. Although God does not always stop evil in the way and time we would expect, He has promised to override evil and use it for His own purposes. We see this happening today before our very eyes.

The Bible is more than just an antiquated land registry book. It is a written record of God's active involvement in human affairs. Although higher critics of the Bible and extreme agnostics reject the notion, the only rational and reasonable explanation for events taking place in our world is that the Lord has a plan for the nations and our lives individually. That plan is to place salvation in Zion from which He will bless the whole world. God is still actively involved in our world to complete His plan.

Consider Theodore Herzl who is rightly acknowledged as the father of modern Zionism. Herzl was an assimilated, secular Jew. Yet, shortly before he died, Herzl told his friend Reuben Brainin that when he was twelve years of age, the King Messiah appeared to him in a dream.

Herzl said of the Messiah:

> He took me in His arms and carried me off on the wings of heaven. On one of the iridescent clouds we met Moses. The Messiah called out to Moses, "For this child I have prayed." To me He said, "Go and announce to the Jews that I shall soon come and perform great and wondrous deeds for My people and for all mankind." Herzl said, "I have kept this dream to myself, and did not dare tell anyone."[17]

Consider General Edmund Allenby, the great Christian general who liberated Jerusalem from the Turks in 1917. As a young Christian boy in England, his mother taught him to end his bedtime prayers with these words, "And, O Lord, we would not forget your ancient people, Israel. Hasten the day when Israel shall again be your people and shall be restored to your favor and to their land." Allenby said, "I never knew God would give me the privilege of answering my own childhood prayer."[18]

Consider Eliezer Ben-Yehuda who is recognized as the father of the modern Hebrew language. He was a young man suffering greatly from tuberculosis. He was jailed as a revolutionary and attacked by his own people. His first wife died, leaving him with small children. He was a secular Jew.

At the age of 20, a light flashed in Eliezer's mind. He heard a voice inside him saying, "It is time for the revival of Israel and its language in the land of it forefathers." When Eliezer tried to describe the moment, he said it was like "lightning before my eyes."[19]

God had promised in Jeremiah 31:23 and Zephaniah 3:9 that He would revive the ancient Hebrew language, and He chose Ben Yehuda to accomplish His work. Even though Ben Yehuda was a secular Jew, the Lord God used Him to fulfill Bible prophecy.

We could consider many others to show the hand of the Lord in the return of the Jews to Israel, even though God might use ordinary people like Herzl, Allenby, Ben-Yehuda, and you and me to accomplish the task.

Mercy on Zion

The writer of Psalm 102 tells us why God is going to arise. He says the Lord is going to arise to have "mercy on Zion." God's mercy is His faithful, steadfast lovingkindness to place salvation in Zion as His means of blessing the whole world.

God is going to have mercy on Zion because the time to favor her has come. Although the world does not recognize it, the Lord is even now in the process of accomplishing this. It's all recorded in the Bible and happening today!

Most people arise from bed each morning because they have something to do that day. They usually set an alarm clock to wake them up at a specific time. People don't just happen to wake up by chance. If they are on vacation and don't have any plans, they may "sleep in."

Because God has a task to accomplish, He has set His divine clock. He is awake. He is not sleeping late. He is now working to place salvation in Zion. The events in our world are not just happening by chance. God has a set time to favor Zion, and that time has come. His heavenly alarm has sounded, and He is actively fulfilling His plans. He is bringing to pass the ancient words of the prophets to establish true "peace for our times."

Personal Study Review

1. Explain the "Time to Favor Zion."
2. Explain why God must build up Zion.
3. Give some examples of God at work in the lives of ordinary people in history.

Chapter 9

Building Up Zion Part 1

The world's "peace process" is based on tearing down Zion. By that I mean weakening or destroying the state of Israel. God's "peace process" is based on building up Zion. This means that God's agenda to bring about world peace is just the opposite of that of world leaders. This presents us with a problem. We have opposing "peace processes." Whose "peace process" do you think will prevail? If you said, "God" then you answered correctly.

No matter how many trips the U.S. State Department makes to Israel, they are not going to achieve peace. Until the nations recognize that the One True God opposes their plans, we will continue to have conflict in the Middle East. But the recognition of this fact in itself will not bring peace. The nations must submit their will to God. If they are not willing to do so of their own free will, God will allow circumstances in our world to go from bad to worse.

In our world today, conflicts have a way of breaking out of their region. Radical Islamists terrorist are not confined to the Middle East. They are everywhere. This means we will never have the blessing of world peace until the leaders of the nations recognize the God of Abraham, Isaac and Jacob as the One True God and accept His peace plan as recorded in the Bible, not the Koran.

The God of the Bible has a plan to bless the world from Zion. He is actively bringing that plan to pass. Since God's peace plan centers on building up Zion, we need to know what it means to "Build up Zion?" What is Zion? What is Zionism? How does God plan to "Build up Zion?" Let's now answer these questions.

THE MEANING OF ZION AND ZIONISM

The word Zion appears in the Bible 159 times. It is found 152 times in the Hebrew Scriptures and 7 times in the New Testament. The word *Zion* most likely means stronghold. It was a Jebusite fortress before King David captured and made it his capital.

> *And David and all Israel went to Jerusalem, which is Jebus, where the Jebusites were, the inhabitants of the land. But the inhabitants of Jebus said to David, "You shall not come in here!" Nevertheless, David took the stronghold of Zion (that is, the City of David.) Now David said, "Whoever attacks the Jebusites first shall be chief and captain." And Joab the son of Zeruiah went up first, and became chief. Then David dwelt in the stronghold; therefore they called it the City of David. And he built the city around it, from the Millo to the surrounding area. Joab repaired the rest of the city. So David went on and became great, and the Lord of hosts was with him.*[1]

Biblical Zion at that time was the southeastern ridge of Mount Zion and was called the City of David. David brought the Ark of the Covenant to Mount Zion where he set up the

Tabernacle of David to worship the Lord. At that time, the Ark of the Covenant was in the house of a man named Obed-Edom. When David learned that the presence of the Ark of the Covenant had blessed Obed-Edom, he went and brought the Ark to the City of David.

> Now it was told King David, saying, "The Lord has blessed the house of Obed-Edom and all that belongs to him, because of the ark of God." So David went and brought up the ark of God from the house of Obed-Edom to the City of David with gladness. So they brought the ark of the Lord, and set it in its place in the midst of the tabernacle that David had erected for it. Then David offered burnt offerings and peace offerings before the Lord.[2]

When King David died, he was succeeded by his son, Solomon. When Solomon became king, he built the Jewish Temple on Mount Moriah. This was around the year 970 B.C. Mount Moriah is the location of the Temple Mount in Jerusalem today. So we see that the Jewish Temple was built on the present Temple Mount about 1,600 years before Mohammed established Islam. Solomon moved the ark there and the name Zion was extended to include the Temple Mount.

> *Now Solomon began to build the house of the Lord at Jerusalem on Mount Moriah, where the Lord had appeared to his father David, at the place where David had prepared on the threshing floor of Ornan the Jebusite. Now Solomon assembled the elders of Israel and all the heads of the tribes, the chief fathers of the children of Israel, in Jerusalem, that they might bring the ark of the covenant of the Lord up from the City of David, which is Zion.*[3]

When Solomon dedicated the Temple to the Lord, the glory of God so filled the Temple that the people could not stand in

His presence. Solomon worshiped the God of Israel and proclaimed that He was the only true God.

> *And it came to pass, when the priests came out of the holy place, that the cloud filled the house of the Lord, so that the priests could not continue ministering because of the cloud; for the glory of the Lord filled the house of the Lord.*[4]

> *Then Solomon stood before the altar of the Lord in the presence of all the assembly of Israel, and spread out his hands toward heaven; and he said, "Lord God of Israel, there is no God in heaven above or on earth below like You, who keep Your covenant and mercy with Your servants who walk before You with all their hearts."*[5]

Later the people worshiped other gods to the point that the presence of the One True God left the Temple. But even then, He promised that at the end of days His presence would return to a rebuilt Temple when the Jews are back in their land in Jerusalem. According to the Hebrew Bible, the glory of the Lord departed the Temple from the Eastern Gate and will return through that same Eastern Gate. The Eastern Gate of the Temple Mount today is at this location.

> *Then the glory of the Lord departed from the threshold of the temple and stood over the cherubim. And the cherubim lifted their wings and mounted up from the earth in my sight. When they went out, the wheels were beside them; and they stood at the door of the east gate of the Lord's house, and the glory of the God of Israel was above them.*[6]

> *And the glory of the Lord came into the temple by way of the gate which faces toward the east. And He said to me, "Son of man, this is the place of my throne and the place of the soles of My feet, where I will dwell in the midst of the children of Israel forever....*[7]

Eventually, Zion referred to the whole of Jerusalem, the land of Israel and the people themselves. It was God's heart cry that His people seek the peace of Zion and Jerusalem because there would never be peace in the world until there was first peace in Jerusalem.

> *For Zion's sake I will not hold My peace, and for Jerusalem's sake I will not rest, until her righteousness goes forth as brightness, and her salvation as a lamp that burns. I have set watchmen on your walls, O Jerusalem; they shall never hold their peace day or night. You who make mention of the Lord, do not keep silent, and give Him no rest till He establishes and till He makes Jerusalem a praise in the earth.*[8]

"Pray for the peace of Jerusalem; may they prosper who love you. Peace be within your walls, prosperity within your palaces. For the sake of my brethren and companions, I will now say, 'Peace be within you.' Because of the house of the Lord our God I will seek your good."[9]

At the end of the age, the Lord promised to return to Zion, at which time He will gather the Jewish people back to their land from all the nations where He had sent them. They would live in Jerusalem, rebuild their Temple and the Jewish Messiah, not the Mahdi, would rule and reign from Zion.

> *Thus says the Lord of hosts: 'I am zealous for Zion with great zeal; with great fervor I am zealous for her.' Thus says the Lord: I will return to Zion, and dwell in the midst of Jerusalem. Jerusalem shall be called the City of Truth, the Mountain of the Lord of hosts, the Holy Mountain.' Thus says the Lord of hosts: 'Old men and old women shall again sit in the streets of Jerusalem, each with his staff in his hand because of great age. The streets of the city shall be full of boys and girls playing in its streets.' Thus says the Lord of hosts: 'Behold, I will save My people from the Land of the east and from the*

land of the west; I will bring them back, and they shall dwell in the midst of Jerusalem. They shall be My people and I will be their God, in truth and righteousness.'[10]

SECULAR ZIONISM

Over the centuries, there developed different understandings of Zion or Zionism. Because of time and history, people reinterpreted *Zion* to mean what they needed it to mean for their own time and agenda. There is the secular Jewish understanding that Zionism is strictly a political movement to establish a national homeland for the Jewish people. Zionism was first applied to this modern movement in 1890 by Nathan Birnbaum, a Jewish philosopher from Austria.[11]

Many excellent books have been written on the birth of Zionism which eventually led to the establishing of the nation of Israel. It is a fascinating story about which we should all be informed.

Theodore Herzl is considered to be the father of modern Zionism. Herzl was born in 1860 in Budapest and was the son of a wealthy banker. Herzl studied law but later became a journalist. He felt very comfortable as an assimilated Jew living in a Gentile world.

Because of the French Revolution emphasizing the brotherhood of man and equality for all, Herzl believed that Gentile hatred of Jews was a thing of the past. He was soon to find out just how deceived he was about the heart of mankind.

In 1894, Herzl had gone to Paris to cover the trial of Alfred Dreyfus, a captain in the French army and a Jew. Dreyfus was accused of giving French military secrets to the Germans and was publicly humiliated and sentenced to life in prison even though there was no evidence against him. This incident became known as the "Dreyfus Affair."

An angry public demanded justice. They shouted, "Kill the traitor, kill the Jew." They didn't particularly believe Dreyfus was guilty, but they used his misfortune to vent their hate for the Jews. When Herzl saw and heard the angry mob demanding Jewish blood, he knew that Gentile hatred of Jews was still part of his world.

With this sobering awakening, Herzl realized the Jewish people would never be safe living among the Gentile nations. In 1896, Herzl wrote *The Jewish State* in which he challenged the Jews to establish their own nation where they would be safe from prejudice and persecution.

One year later, in 1897, Herzl organized the First Zionist Congress which met in Basil, Switzerland. The Congress was attended by 204 delegates. They lit the fires of Zionism in the hearts of Jews, stated their intentions to establish a Jewish state, designed the Jewish flag, and wrote the song that would eventually become the national anthem of Israel, "Hatikvah" (The Hope).

The moving words to that anthem say:

So long as still within our breasts
The Jewish heart beats true,
So long as still toward the East,
To Zion, looks the Jew,
So long as our hopes are not yet lost—
Two thousand years we cherished them—
To live in freedom in the land
Of Zion and Jerusalem

At this conference, Herzl predicted that the Jews would have their own state in 50 years or less.[12] Was it a coincidence or the hand of the Lord that brought forth the fulfillment of Herzl's prediction when, exactly fifty years later on November 29, 1947, the United Nations agreed to the establishing of a homeland for the Jews in what was then called Palestine?

The Zionist Congress platform stated their aim was to create a publicly recognized, legally secured home for the Jewish people in Palestine.

Max Nordau, who had been one of the delegates and became a spokesman for the movement, said:

> The New Zionism, which has been called political, differs from the old, religious, messianic variety in that it disavows all mysticism, no longer identifies itself with messianism, and does not expect the return to Palestine to be brought about by a miracle, but desires to prepare the way by its own efforts.[13]

Because this platform, as well as most of the early pioneers of Zionism, was secular, many think the existence of the state of Israel is merely a human work in which the Jews "just got lucky." People fail to see God's providence in using them for His purposes.

Yet, Moses, of all people spoke of this latter day ingathering and said:

> *Then the Lord your God will bring you to the land which your fathers possessed, and you shall possess it. He will prosper you and multiply you more than your fathers. And the Lord your God will circumcise your heart and the heart of your descendants, to love the Lord your God with all your heart and with all your soul, that you may live.*[14]

REPLACEMENT THEOLOGY ZIONISM

A second understanding of Zion and Zionism is called "Replacement Theology." This view, held by many Christians is strictly a spiritual one. Proponents of Replacement Theology believe that the Christian church has replaced the Jewish people and Israel in God's plan of redemption. In their view, the church is the "New Israel and Zion." Nothing could be further from the truth.

In my book, *How the Cross became a Sword*, I explained the origin of this teaching and the deadly fruit it has produced in fostering anti-Semitism down through the ages. Replacement Theology had its beginnings at the first Christian Seminary in Alexandria, Egypt. Because of the Greek culture at Alexandria, the Christian school of learning used the Greek allegorical method of interpreting the Hebrew Scriptures.

The first head of the school was a man named Pantaenus. He was succeeded by Clement who served as the head of the school and its chief instructor from about A.D. 180 to A.D. 202 Clement laid the foundation built on by his successors which established Replacement Theology as the generally accepted teaching of the church for centuries.

Clement was succeeded by a man named Origen. Origen was perhaps the greatest scholar of his day. His knowledge of philosophy and theology were unparalleled. His fame and influence was recognized throughout the Roman world.

Origen taught the allegorical method of interpreting the Hebrew Scriptures. This method of interpretation denies the literal meaning of the text. Origen's views were accepted by his colleagues, and became the standard for the church. It is this system that produced the teaching that the church is Zion which has replaced literal Israel in the plan and purposes of God. The allegorical method of interpretation laid the foundation for anti-Semitism in the church that was built on by successive generations until the Puritan revival in the 1600s.

Jesus said a tree is known by its fruit (Matt. 7:16-20). The fruit of Replacement Theology is a prideful arrogance and hatred toward the Jewish people that is clearly contrary to God's Word and true Christian character. Hitler plucked this fruit from the writings of church leaders and used it to justify the Holocaust.

The apostle Paul refuted this teaching with these words:

> *I say then, has God cast away His people? Certainly not!... do not boast against the branches* [the Jews]. *But if you do boast, remember that you* [the Gentiles] *do not support the root, but the root supports you.*[15]

The God of the Bible made a literal, binding, unconditional, everlasting covenant with Abraham and his descendants to give them the promised land, make them the head nation on the earth, and bless the world through the Jewish Messiah.

Although any one generation of Jews might miss the blessings and benefits of this covenant because of their sin, the covenant itself continues from one generation to the next until the time to favor Zion comes. At that time, the Lord will completely fulfill His covenant promise to Abraham. We are living in that time period. A person has to be completely ignorant of the Bible or disbelieve it not to realize the Lord is behind the scenes moving the course of events to fulfill His ancient promises in the Bible.

BIBLICAL ZIONISM

This brings us to the third understanding of Zion—the biblical understanding. Biblical Zion is both a natural and a spiritual movement. *Biblical Zionism* can be defined as the return of the Jewish people to their national and spiritual roots as revealed in the Bible in preparation for the coming of the Jewish Messiah.

A biblical Zionist is simply a person who believes the biblical promises God made to Abraham, Isaac, and Jacob to give them and their descendants the land of Israel as an everlasting possession. Biblical Zionists understand that the God of the Bible chose the ancient nation of Israel to reveal His plan for the redemption of the world and that the modern ingathering of the Jewish people back to their land is a sovereign work of God in fulfillment of Bible prophecy. Anyone who believes this, be they Jew or Gentile, is a Zionist who should labor with God for its fulfillment by actively participating in the process.

While the Bible predicts that the Jews would be exiled from their Land, as history has proven true, it also says that the God of Israel would preserve a remnant of His people and bring them back to their Promised Land. Since the prophecy of the exile has proven to be true, should rational thinking people also expect the prophecy of the return to be true?

The Scriptures given below are just a few of many which we could provide. There is no way a person can read these verses with their plain meaning and not understand God's intentions. We may not like His intentions, but we can certainly understand them.

God's Covenant with Abraham

...Get out of your country, from your family and from your father's house; to a land that I will show you. I will make you a great nation; I will bless you and make your name great; and you shall be a blessing. I will bless those who bless you, and I will curse him who curses you; and in you all the families of the earth shall be blessed.[16]

...To your descendants I will give this land.[17]

...Lift your eyes now and look from the place where you areænorthward, southward, eastward and westward; for all the land which you see I give to you and your descendents forever...Arise, walk in the land through its length and its width, for I give it to you.[18]

On the same day the Lord made a covenant with Abraham, saying: "To your descendants I have given this land, from the river of Egypt to the great river, the river Euphrates."[19]

And I will establish My covenant between Me and you and your descendants after you in their generations, for an everlasting covenant, to be God to you and your descendants after you. Also I give to you and your descendants after you the land in which you are a stranger, all the land of Canaan, as an everlasting possession; and I will be their God.[20]

The Covenant Confirmed With Isaac

And Abraham said to God, 'Oh, that Ishmael might live before You!' Then God said, 'No, Sarah your wife shall bear you a son, and you shall call his name Isaac; I will establish My covenant with him for an everlasting covenant, and with his descendants after him.'[21]

The Covenant Promise to Jacob (Israel)

...I am the Lord God of Abraham your father and the God of Isaac; the land on which you lie I will give it to you and your descendants. Also your descendants shall be as the dust of the earth; you shall spread abroad to the west and the east, to the north and the south; and in you and in your seed all the families of the earth shall be blessed.[22]

God promised the covenant would be perpetual in spite of the failures of His ancient people to obey Him:

"Remember His covenant forever, the word which He commanded for a thousand generations, the covenant which He made with Abraham, and His oath to Isaac, and confirmed it to Jacob for a statute, to Israel for an everlasting covenant."[23]

Ezekiel believed he was speaking for the Lord when he wrote:

...Thus says the Lord God: 'Although I have cast them far off among the Gentiles, and although I have scattered them among the countries, yet I shall be a little sanctuary from them in the countries where they have gone....I will gather you

> *from the peoples, assemble you from the countries where you have been scattered, and I will give you the land of Israel.'*[24]

There are different views on the details of this "Jewish homecoming." Some believe this ingathering to be a work of the Messiah while others understand that more conventional human efforts will bring about the ingather of the exiles. Still others see a combination of the two with the hand of the Almighty working through human efforts to realize the age-old cry of the Jewish people, "Next Year in Jerusalem."

No matter how they may differ on details, Biblical Zionists understand the present ingathering of the Jewish people to Israel as a fulfillment of the biblical prophecies. Throughout their two thousand year exile, the Jewish people have prayed for this return as expressed in the tenth blessing of their great prayer, the *Amidah*. It says, "Sound the great shofar for our freedom, raise the banner to gather the exiles and gather us from the four corners of the earth. Blessed are You, Hashem, who gathers in the dispersed of His people Israel."[25]

The yearning to rebuild Jerusalem is also found in the fourteenth blessing of the Amidah which says:

> And to Jerusalem, Your city, may You return in compassion, and may You rest within it, as you have spoken. May you rebuild it soon in our days as an eternal structure, and may You speedily establish the throne of David within it. Blessed are You, Hashem, the Builder of Jerusalem.[26]

Because God has chosen Zion does not mean He is anti-Arab. God loves the Arab people the same as He does the Jewish people. His plan is a matter of His choice, not His love. Even so, we must understand that God has different plans for the nations just as He has different plans for our individual lives.

The Lord has a wonderful plan to bless the Arab people, as we learn from these words given to us by the prophet Isaiah, "In that day there will be a highway from Egypt to Assyria, and the Assyrian will come into Egypt and the Egyptian to Assyria, and the Egyptians will serve with the Assyrians.

"In that day Israel will be one of three with Egypt and Assyriaæa blessing in the midst of the land, whom the Lord of hosts shall bless, saying, 'Blessed is Egypt My people, and Assyria the work of My hands, and Israel My inheritance.'"[27]

When the Arab nations stop fighting Israel and recognize God's plans for them, they will be greatly blessed, for God loves them as well and desires to bless them. However, He cannot bless them as long as they oppose His purpose to place salvation in Zion. Therefore, biblical Zionists should show love to the Arab people and pray for them to come into agreement with God's agenda.

CHRISTIAN ZIONISM

Bible believing Christians are biblical Zionists. They are generally referred to as Christian Zionist. Christian Zionists believe that the God of the Bible made an everlasting covenant with Abraham, Isaac and Jacob, which is still in force today. Part of that covenant, which we have just seen, includes the promise of the land that would eventually be called Zion or Israel. Christian Zionist believes that the modern ingathering of the Jewish people back to their land is a work of God that will bless the whole world. To the contrary, opposing this work of God will continue to bring more wars and more suffering.

Zionism and Zionist are words that technically relate to Jews. However, at the first Zionist Congress in 1897, Theodore Herzl acknowledged his Gentile friends attending the Congress as "Christian Zionist." From that time until now, Jewish and

Christian Zionists have worked together to fulfill the centuries old dream of "Next Year in Jerusalem."

Christian Zionism actually pre-dates Herzl. The Puritans published many books in the 16th and 17th century declaring that one day the Jews would return to their ancient land.

In addition, there were many influential Christian Zionists in England and America in the 1800s. Lord Shaftesbury, who led the abolition of slavery in England, proposed the return of the Jews to Palestine under the supervision of the British government. Jean Dunant, the founder of the International Red Cross, established the Palestine Colonial Company to assist Jews in making *Aliyah*.

William Hechler was the Anglican minister who opened doors for Herzl and won support from the Church of England for sponsoring the return of the Jews to Palestine. The result was the *Balfour Declaration* written by Christian Zionist, James Balfour.

American minister William Blackstone sent petitions to the United States government requesting American support for the return of the Jews to Palestine. Many prominent American leaders signed the petition.

Christian Zionist organizations in our time are working tirelessly on behalf of the Jewish people and the people of Israel. For this reason, radical Islamist have called Christian Zionist their enemy.

Christian Zionists do not consider the Arab-Israeli conflict a political issue. They consider it a spiritual issue with political consequences that goes to the very core of the biblical revelation of the God of Israel, the integrity of God's holy Word, and the existence of the Jewish people as the covenant people of God. Christian Zionists take God at His word when He says:

> *'I will bring back the captives of My people Israel; they shall build the waste cities and inhabit them; they shall plant vineyards and drink wine from them; they shall also make gardens and eat fruit from them. I will plant them in their land, and no longer shall they be pulled up from the land I have given them,' says the Lord your God.*[28]

It is tragic that the church has failed to recognize this important aspect of God's redemptive plans and purposes for Jews and Christians to work together for the cause of Zion. Not only has the church failed to understand this work of God, it has fought against it for most of the entire history of Christianity. However, God will accomplish His purposes in spite of the ignorance and indifference of His people. He has awakened many thousands of true believers around the world to their responsibility to stand in solidarity with the people of Israel.

Personal Study Review

1. Explain the meaning of Zion and Zionism.
2. Explain Secularism Zionism.
3. Explain "Replacement Theology."
4. Explain Biblical Zionism.
5. Explain Christian Zionism.

Chapter 10

BUILDING UP ZION PART 2

In spite of the plans of Islamic Jihad and the nations of the world, the One True God is going to fulfill His covenant word and promises to Abraham, Isaac and Jacob. He is going to build up Zion. In fact, God is already doing this. One would have to be totally ignorant or willingly turn a blind eye to the on-going work of God in our times to build up Zion.

While Israel is continually vilified as the source of suffering of all mankind, her contributions to the betterment of the world are ignored. The world has been blessed beyond measure through the Jewish people in the *Diaspora* and the people of Israel. Not only have the Jewish people blessed the world with moral and spiritual truths and values, they have also dramatically improved the quality of life for all mankind.

Israel is the one of the 100 smallest countries in the world with less than 1/1000th of the world's population. Yet her contributions to make the world a better place far exceed her numbers and resources. I have listed some of her more significant achievements below along with achievements by Jews living outside of Israel. I first wrote this for an article published by the *Jewish Herald Voice* newspaper in Houston, Texas.[1]

1. In spite of their few numbers, Jews have received 126 Nobel Prizes, including 43 for medicine. This represents over 20% of all awards worldwide during the 20th century. (As a young boy growing up in the '40s and '50s, I am especially grateful to the Jewish doctor Jonas Salk who gave me and the world a polio vaccine that immunized us from this terrible disease.)

2. In chemistry, Jews have been honored with 28 Nobel Prizes, which is 19% of the world total and 28% of the U.S. total.

3. In economics, Jews have received 21 Nobel Prizes, which is 38% of the world total and 53% of the U.S. total.

4. In literature, Jews have received 12 Nobel Prizes, which is 12% of the world total and 27% of the U.S. total.

5. In physiology and medicine, Jews have received 52 Nobel Prizes, which is 29% of the world total and 42% of the U.S. total.

6. In contributions to world peace, Jews have received 9 Nobel Prizes, which is 10% of the world total and 11% of the U.S. total.

7. In physics, Jews have received 45 Nobel Prizes, which is 26% of the world total and 30% of the U.S. total.

8. Israel leads the world in the number of scientists and technicians in the workforce with 145 per 10,000, as compared to 85 per 10,000 in the United States, 70

per 10,000 in Japan and less that 60 per 10,000 in Germany.

9. Israel leads the world with over 25% of its workforce employed in technical professions.
10. In proportion to its population, Israel has the largest number of startup companies in the world and the highest concentration of hi-tech companies in the world outside of Silicon Valley. (On a recent vacation, my wife and I joined a small group that hooked themselves to a cable and "zipped" high above the trees across the jungle. One of my "zipping partners" worked for a venture capital firm in Boston that specializes in investments in Israel. Now imagine zipping high in the air across the jungle (don't look down) while discussing your latest trips to Israel).
11. The cell phone was developed in Israel by Motorola-Israel.
12. Intel researchers in Israel recently announced a new computer chip technology that will speed up the flow of data to the speed of light which will revolutionize computing and telecommunications.
13. Most of the Windows NT and XP operating systems were developed by Microsoft-Israel.
14. The Pentium MMX Chip, the Pentium-4 microprocessor and the Centrino processor were designed, developed and produced by Intel in Israel.
15. The technology for the AOL Instant Messenger was developed in 1996 by four young Israelis.
16. Israel's Weizmann Institute recently announced the world's smallest computer to diagnose cancer. It is

made up entirely of biological molecules and is about a trillionth the size of a drop of water.

17. Israel's $100 billion economy is larger than all of its immediate neighbors combined.
18. Israel has the highest living standards in the Middle East with per capita far exceeding her Arab neighbors.
19. Twenty-four percent of Israel's workforce holds university degrees, ranking third after the U.S. and Holland.
20. Israel has the world's second highest per capita of new books and more museums per capita than any other country.
21. Israel has the highest percentage in the world of home computer per capita.
22. Israel has the highest ratio of university degrees to the population in the world.
23. Israel produces more scientific papers per capita than any other nation—109 per 10,000 people.
24. Israel has one of the highest per capita of patents filed.
25. Israel has the world's second highest per capita of new books.
26. Israel had developed many products in the medical field such as instrumentation to detect breast cancer, proper administration of medicine, the first ingestible video camera, a new device that helps the heart pump blood, etc., etc., etc.
27. Israel's development of drip irrigation and biotechnology has aided agricultural development in arid regions of the world.

28. Israel has found ways to make the desert bloom. She raises fish in the desert, ships flowers to the Netherlands and exports food to her neighbors.

In spite of all these incredible accomplishments, the French Ambassador in England has said that "Israel is nothing but a #*&*# little country."

At an address to Nefesh B' Nefesh, the organization that helps Jews from America to make *Aliyah*, Binyamin Netanyahu told the new immigrants their choice to make *Aliyah* was a harbinger of change for the entire Zionist enterprise. "You will witness in your lifetimes a monumental shift," he said, "not seen since biblical times and the days of the Second Temple; the majority of Jews will live in the Jewish state."

Noting the prevalence of intermarriage in the Diaspora and the general erosion of Jewish identity there, Netanyah added, "For half a century, the survival and future of Israel depended on *Aliyah*. In the next half-century, however the survival and future of the Jewish people will depend on the State of Israel."[2]

Zion Regathered

God's plan to build up Zion involves three phases that are now happening in the following sequence. These are: 1) Regathering, 2) Redeeming, and 3) Restoring. There are many places in the Bible where the Lord says He will regather the Jewish people to their ancient homeland for the purpose of making them a great nation while preparing them for the coming of the Messiah. Even now the Interior Ministry in Israel is preparing for a population of 12 million Jews in Israel.

Of course if a person does not believe the Bible or believes the Bible has been corrupted and superseded by the Koran, these verses from the Bible mean nothing. However, for Christians and Jews who believe the Bible, he or she must determine what this means for his or her life. I have listed below just a few of the many Scriptures which speak of this great ingathering. We have read some of them in earlier chapters.

> *The Lord your God will bring you back from captivity, and have compassion on you, and gather you again from all the nations where the Lord your God has scattered you. If any of you are driven out to the farthest parts under heaven, from there the Lord your God will gather you, and from there He will bring you. Then the Lord your God will bring you to the land which your fathers possessed, and you shall posses it. He will prosper you and multiply you more than your fathers. And the Lord your God will circumcise your heart and the heart of your descendants, to love the Lord your God with all your heart and with all your soul, that you may live.*[3]

> *He will set up a banner for the nations, and will assemble the outcasts of Israel, and gather together the dispersed of Judah from the four corners of the earth.*[4]

> *Fear not, for I am with you; I will bring your descendants from the east, and gather you from the west, I will say to the north, 'Give them up!' and to the south, 'Do not keep them back!' Bring My sons from afar, and My daughters from the ends of the earth.*[5]

> *For I will set My eyes on them for good, and I will bring them back to this land; I will build them and not pull them down, and I will plant them and not pluck them up. Then I will give them a heart to know Me, that I am the Lord; and they shall be My people, and I will be their God, for they shall return to Me with their whole heart.*[6]

> *Hear the word of the Lord, O nations, and declare it in the isles afar off, and say, "He who scattered Israel will gather him, and keep him as a shepherd does his flock."*[7]

Thus says the Lord God: "Although I have cast them far off among the Gentiles, and although I have scattered them among the countries, yet I shall be a little sanctuary for them in the countries where they have gone…I will gather you from the peoples, assemble you from the countries where you have been scattered, and I will give you the land of Israel …Then I will give them one heart, and I will put a new spirit within them, and take the stony heart out of their flesh, that they may walk in My statutes and keep My judgments and do them; and they shall be My people, and I will be their God."[8]

"I will bring back the captives of My people Israel; they shall build the waste cities and inhabit them; they shall plant vineyards and drink wine from them; they shall also make gardens and eat fruit from them. I will plant them in their land, and no longer shall they be pulled from the land I have given them," says the Lord your God.[9]

But Zion said, "The Lord has forsaken me, and my Lord has forgotten me. Can a woman forget her nursing child, and not have compassion on the son of her womb? Surely they may forget, yet I will not forget you. See, I have inscribed [carved] *you on the palms of My hands; your walls are always before Me. For your waste and desolate places, and the land of your destruction, will even now be too small for the inhabitants; and those who swallowed you up will be far away. The children you will have, after you have lost the others, will say again in your ears, 'The place is too small for me; give me a place where I may dwell.'"*[10]

For Zion's sake I will not hold My peace, and for Jerusalem's sake I will not rest, until her righteousness goes forth as brightness, and her salvation as a lamp that burns. You shall no longer be termed Forsaken, nor shall your land any more be termed Desolate; But you shall be called Hephzibah, and your land Beulah; for the Lord delights in you, and your land shall be married. For as a young man marries a virgin, so shall your sons marry you; and as the bridegroom rejoices over the bride, so shall your God rejoice over you.[11]

I have set watchman on your walls, O Jerusalem; they shall never hold their peace day or night. You who make mention of the Lord, do not keep silent, and give Him no rest till He establishes and till He makes Jerusalem a praise in the earth.[12]

God has a special word to Christians among the nations to partner with God by assisting the Jewish people in their return to the land.

Isaiah writes these words to believers living at the time when God shows favor to Zion, "Thus says the Lord God: Behold, I will lift My hand in an oath to the nations, and set up My standard for the peoples; they shall bring your sons in their arms and your daughters shall be carried on their shoulders."[13]

Surely the coastlands shall wait for Me; and the ships of Tarshish will come first, to bring your sons from afar, their silver and their gold with them, to the name of the Lord your God, and to the Holy One of Israel, because He has glorified you.[14]

In the New Testament, Jesus gave these words to His followers:

Come, you blessed of My Father, inherit the kingdom prepared for you from the foundation of the world: for I was hungry and you gave Me food; I was thirsty and you gave Me drink; I was a stranger and you took Me in; I was naked and you clothed Me; I was sick and you visited Me; I was in prison and you came to Me. Then the righteous will answer Him saying, "Lord, when did we see You hungry and feed You, or thirsty and give You drink? When did we see You a stranger and take You in, or naked and clothe You? Or when did we see You sick, or in prison, and come to You?" And the King will answer and say to

> *them, "Assuredly, I say to you, inasmuch as you did it to one of the least of these My brethren, you did it to Me."*[15]

ZION REDEEMED

As the Lord regathers His ancient people to the land He promised them, He will also redeem them fully and completely beyond what many have already experienced. While only God knows what is in a person's heart, He has saved the best for last for His covenant people. God has heard their cries for deliverance from their enemies. He is going to bless them with material and spiritual blessing beyond measure that will bless the whole world.

Throughout the Hebrew Scriptures, God says He will redeem both the land and the people. He is not only calling them back to their land, He is also calling them back to Himself to know Him in a most intimate way.

Moses and the prophets spoke of this time when God would bring the Jewish back to their land. He said that God would also circumcise their hearts to love Him in a much more personal way than many may have understood and experienced. A few relevant Scriptures are listed below.

> *The Lord your God will bring you to the land which your fathers possessed, and you shall posses it. He will prosper you and multiply you more than your fathers. And the Lord your God will circumcise your heart and the heart of your descendants, to love the Lord your God with all your soul, that you may live.*[16]

The prophets gave even more details of this time when God would fully redeem the land and the people. We are seeing these prophecies being fulfilled in our times. For Christians and Jews, it is not a time to fear those who would destroy us. It is a time to have faith and hope in the faithfulness of the God of the Bible to fulfill His covenant promises. The following words of the prophets speak of our times.

> *For the Lord will comfort Zion, He will comfort all her waste places; He will make her wilderness like Eden, and her desert like the garden of the Lord; joy and gladness will be found in it, thanksgiving and the voice of melody. So the randsomed of the Lord shall return, and come to Zion with singing, with everlasting joy on their heads. They shall obtain joy and gladness; sorrow and sighing* [mourning] *shall flee away.*[17]

> *Break forth into joy, sing together, you waste places of Jerusalem! For the Lord has comforted His people, He has redeemed Jerusalem.*[18]

> *Behold, the days are coming, says the Lord, when I will make a new covenant with the house of Israel and with the house of Judah—not according to the covenant that I made with their fathers in the day that I took them by the hand to lead them out of the land of Egypt, My covenant which they broke, though I was a husband to them, says the Lord. But this is the covenant that I will make with the house of Israel after those days, says the Lord: I will put My law in their minds, and write it on their hearts; and I will be their God and they shall be My people.*

> *No more shall every man teach his neighbor, and every man his brother, saying, "Know the Lord," for they shall all know Me, from the least of them to the greatest of them, says the Lord. For I will forgive their iniquity and their sin I will remember no more.*[19]

> *Behold, I will gather them out of all countries where I have driven them in My anger, in My fury, and in great wrath; I will bring them back to this place, and I will cause them to dwell safely. They shall be My people and I shall be their God; then I will give them one heart and one way, that they*

may fear Me forever, for the good of them and their children after them. And I will make an everlasting covenant with them, that I will not turn away from doing them good; but I will put My fear in their hearts so that they will not depart from Me. Yes, I will rejoice over them to do them good, and I will assuredly plant them in this land, with all My heart and with all My soul.[20]

For I will take you from among the nations, gather you out of all countries, and bring you into your own land. Then I will sprinkle clean water on you, and you shall be clean; I will cleanse you from all your filthiness and from all your idols. I will give you a new heart and put a new spirit within you; I will take the heart of stone out of your flesh and give you a heart of flesh. I will put My Spirit within you and cause you to walk in My statutes, and you will keep My judgments and do them. Then you shall dwell in the land that I gave to your fathers; you shall be My people and I will be your God.[21]

"I will put My Spirit in you, and you shall live, and I will place you in your own land. Then you shall know that I, the Lord have spoken it and performed it," says the Lord.[22]

O Israel, hope in the Lord; for with the Lord there is mercy, and with Him is abundant redemption. And He shall redeem Israel from all his iniquities.[23]

"The Redeemer will come to Zion, and to those who turn from transgression in Jacob," says the Lord.[24]

...All flesh shall know that I, the Lord, am your Savior, and your Redeemer, the Mighty One of Jacob.[25]

Say to the daughter of Zion, surely your salvation is coming; behold His reward is with Him, and His work before Him. And they shall call them the Holy People, the Redeemed of the Lord; and you shall be called Sought Out, A City Not Forsaken.[26]

In the New Testament, Jesus spoke of these days and said, "Now when these things begin to happen, look up and lift up your heads, because your redemption draws near.[27]

ZION RESTORED

The third and final phase of building up Zion is restoration. After God regathers and redeems Zion, He will restore to Zion and the Jewish people the full covenant blessings He promised to Abraham, Isaac and Jacob and their descendants. He will do this through the personal presence of the King-Messiah. This is the golden age about which the prophets spoke when King-Messiah will rule the nations from Jerusalem.

Some relevant passages from the Bible are as follows.

Arise, shine; for your light has come! And the glory of the Lord is risen upon you. For behold, the darkness shall cover the earth, and deep darkness the people; but the Lord will arise over you, and His glory will be seen upon you. The Gentiles shall come to your light, and kings to the brightness of your rising. And they shall call you The City of the Lord, Zion of the Holy One of Israel.[28]

At that time Jerusalem shall be called The Throne of the Lord, and all the nations shall be gathered to it, to the name of the Lord, to Jerusalem. No more shall they follow the dictates of their evil hearts.[29]

Now it shall come to pass in the latter days that the mountain of the Lord's house shall be established on the top of the mountains, and shall be exalted above the hills; and all nations shall flow to it. Many people shall come and say, "Come, and let us go up to the mountain of the Lord, to the house of the God of Jacob; He will teach us His ways, and we shall walk in His paths." For out of Zion shall go forth the law, and the word of the Lord from Jerusalem. He shall judge between the nations, and rebuke many people; they shall beat their swords into plowshares, and their spears into pruning hooks; nation shall not lift up sword against nation, neither shall they learn war anymore.[30]

"In that day," says the Lord, "I will assemble the lame, I will gather the outcast and those whom I have afflicted; I will make the lame a remnant, and the outcast a strong nation; so the Lord will reign over them in Mount Zion..."[31]

The Lord will again comfort Zion, and will again choose Jerusalem.... Jerusalem shall be called the City of Truth, the Mountain of the Lord, the Holy Mountain. Behold I will save My people from the land of the east and from the land of the west; I will bring them back, and they shall dwell in the midst of Jerusalem. They shall be My people and I will be their God.... In those days, ten men from every language of the nations shall grasp the sleeve [Tzitzit] *of a Jewish man, saying, "Let us go with you, for we have heard that God is with you."*[32]

The Latter Days

The Bible tells us historically when we can expect to see Zion regathered, redeemed and restored. God's holy Word tells us it will be in the latter days of our present age. When we see Israel renewed, we can know we are living in the latter days leading up to the coming of the Messiah.

The following Scriptures are instructive.

When you are in distress, and all these things come upon you in the latter days, when you turn to the Lord your God and obey His voice (for the Lord your God is a merciful God), He will not forsake you, nor destroy you nor forsake the covenant of your fathers which He swore to them.[33]

In the latter days you will consider it.[34]

For the children of Israel shall abide many days without king or prince, without sacrifice or sacred pillar, without ephod or teraphim. Afterward the children of Israel shall return and seek the Lord their God and David their king. They shall fear the Lord and His goodness in the latter days.[35]

Now I have come to make you understand what will happen in the latter years when Israel is once again a nation.[36]

Oh, that the salvation of Israel would come out of Zion! When the Lord brings back the captivity of His people, let Jacob rejoice and Israel be glad.[37]

In the New Testament, Jesus said: "...Jerusalem will be trampled by Gentiles until the times of the Gentiles are fulfilled."[38]

What did Jesus mean by the phrase, "times of the Gentiles?" The times of the Gentiles represents that period of time in world history when the Gentile nations would rule over Jerusalem and dominate the Jewish people. God would allow this as part of His sovereignty over the flow of world history in working out His divine plans and purposes.

When one of these nations or empires had served its purpose, God would allow its destruction and raise up another in its place. This cycle would continue through the course of world history until God would bring it to a close with the coming of the Jewish Messiah in power and glory.

Gentile domination of world affairs would be characterized by unrighteousness and hatred of the Jews. In the last days, this unrighteousness and hatred would run its course and God would bring it to an end through the Messiah who would establish

God's righteous rule on the earth. Messiah would administer His rule through the nation of Israel as the head nation on the earth, thus ending the time of the Gentiles. We are clearly living in this time period.

The writer of Psalm 102 was thinking about our times when he said the time to favor Zion has come. He went on to say:

> *This will be written for the generation to come, that a people yet to be created may praise the Lord. To declare the name of the Lord in Jerusalem, when the peoples are gathered together, and the kingdoms, to serve the Lord.*[39]

The Hebrew expression for the English phrase, generation to come can literally be translated as, "Let this be written for the last generation."[40] The last generation is the people who are living to see Zion renewed in preparation for the coming of the Messiah.

In the New Testament, the disciples of Jesus, who were all Jewish, asked Him what would be the sign of His coming and the end of the age (Matt. 24:3). Jesus gave a long answer predicting future events. He then said:

> *Now learn this parable from the fig tree: when its branch has already become tender and puts forth leaves, you know that summer is near. So you also, when you see all these things, know it is near—at the doors! at the doors! Assuredly, I say to you, this generation will by no means pass away till all these things take place. Heaven and earth will pass away, but My words will by no means pass away.*[41]

Jesus spoke a parable using the fig tree as a symbol of the renewal of Israel. Then, perhaps with Psalm 102:18 in mind, He said the generation of people who witnessed this would be the last generation living at the time of His coming.

The Bible tells us, "To everything there is a season, a time for every purpose under heaven."[42] As we see Israel renewed before our very eyes, we can knowæthe time to favor Zion has come!

Personal Study Review

1. Explain Zion regathered.
2. Explain Zion redeemed.
3. Explain Zion restored.
4. What might this mean for the world we live in today?
5. What might this mean for your own life?

Chapter 11

Christians and the Arab-Israeli Conflict Part 1

How should Christians respond to the Arab-Israeli conflict? What is our position? Before answering these questions, we must learn the truth about the conflict between Israel and her Arab neighbors. There are so many different voices claiming to speak the truth. Some speak from a hidden agenda. Some raise voices of hate, while others are well meaning, but uninformed. How can we know which ones to believe?

Like all people of goodwill, Christians are deeply concerned about truth, justice and compassion. We desire that people be given the opportunity to live with honor, dignity, freedom and peace. We truly want to listen to every legitimate voice that shares these values. There are a number of voices that speak clearly and truthfully to the Arab-Israeli conflict. Perhaps they can help clarify some of the issues.

The Voice of Scripture

As "People of the Book," Christians and Jews should look to God's holy word as the voice of truth regarding the problems between Israel, the PLO, and the surrounding Moslem and Arab countries. What does the voice of Scripture say?

I have quoted many Bible verses in the previous chapters that state God's intentions concerning the land. For the sake of continuity, and so we can clearly hear the voice of Scripture, I am repeating some of them in the text below.

Approximately 4,000 years ago, the God of the Bible made an eternal covenant decree in which He gave the Promised Land to Abraham and his descendants. This is recorded many times in the Bible so that there would be no confusion about the will of the Almighty concerning the land. Those who refuse to hear this voice do so at their own peril.

As we have already read, the Lord said to Abraham:

> *And I will establish My covenant between Me and you and your descendants after you in their generations, for an everlasting covenant, to be God to you and your descendants after you. Also I give to you and your descendants after you the land in which you are a stranger; and I will be their God.*[1]

When Abraham fathered Ishmael, he believed that God's promises would extend to him. While the Lord promised to bless Ishmael (Genesis 16:10), He made it clear that His covenant to Abraham regarding the Promised Land would be passed to Isaac and Jacob, not Ishmael and Esau.

Furthermore, God stated that His covenant promise and oath would be forever in time. It would not be superseded by Christianity or Islam as we learn from the voice of Scripture:

> *He remembers His covenant forever, the word which He commanded, for a thousand generations, the covenant which He made with Abraham, and His oath to Isaac, and confirmed it to Jacob for a statute, to Israel as an everlasting covenant, saying, "To you I will give the land of Canaan as the allotment of your inheritance."*[2]

It is important we understand that God was not against Ishmael (Genesis 21:17-18). However, His covenant promise of the land was to the Jewish people. This is an eternal decree that God is still honoring.

Likewise, Christians supporting Israel does not mean that we are anti-Arab. As I have said earlier and tried to make clear, the Lord loves all people the same and so should we. But we must recognize that the Almighty has different plans and purposes for different people groups. We will not have peace in this world until the nations acknowledge that the God of Israel is the One True God and submit to His peace plan. When the Lord builds up Zion, His blessings will go out of Zion to all the nations of the world. Then the utopian world the prophets wrote about will be a reality and nations will beat their swords into plowshares and study war no more (Isaiah 2:1-4).

Christian support of Israel does not mean that we agree with all that Israel says and does. However, Christians must listen to the voice of Scripture as the voice of truth regarding the conflict between Israel and her Arab neighbors.

While wanting the Lord's best for both Jews and Arabs, Christians understand this can only happen when Jews and Arabs recognize God's will regarding the land of Israel. This is why Christians must support Israel in her quest to live in peace with secure borders and Jerusalem as her God-given undivided capital. While we must show compassion to all people, we cannot compromise our beliefs for political correctness.

THE VOICE OF THE PROPHETS

Another major provision of God's covenant with the Jewish people is His promise to return them to the land of Israel from all the nations where they have been scattered. What does the voice of the prophets say about Israel as a nation today? While there were many prophetic voices that spoke of this ingathering, let us hear the voice of Ezekiel.

The voice of Ezekiel was loud and clear regarding God's plan to bring the Jewish people back home to their ancient land. We heard his voice earlier, but let's listen again.

> *...Although I have cast them far off among the Gentiles, and although I have scattered them among the countries, yet I shall be a little sanctuary for them in the countries where they have gone. Therefore, say, "Thus says the Lord God: I will gather you from the peoples, assemble you from the countries where you have been scattered, and I will give you the land of Israel."*[3]

We have also heard the voice of Amos. He was just as loud and clear as Ezekiel when the Lord spoke through him and said:

> *"I will bring back the captives of My people Israel; they shall build the waste cities and inhabit them, they shall plant vineyards and drink wine from them; they shall also make gardens and eat fruit from them. I will plant them in the land, and no longer shall they be pulled up from the land I have given them," says the Lord your God.*[4]

The Lord has certainly kept His promise. In fact, the prophets said the return of the Jews to Israel, their ancient homeland, would be greater than their exodus from Egypt. Consider the exodus of Jews from the former Soviet Union where around a million have come to Israel in just a ten year period.

> *Listen to the voice of Jeremiah, "Therefore behold, the days are coming," says the Lord, "that it shall no more be said, but, ' the*

> *Lord lives who brought up the children from the land of Egypt,' but the 'Lord lives who brought up the children of Isreal from the land of the north and from all the lands where He had driven them.' For I will bring them back into the land which I gave their fathers."*[5]

How can we understand the existence of the state of Israel apart from the voice of Scripture and the prophets? How can we explain that tiny little Israel, about the size of the state of New Jersey, U.S., could win all her wars against impossible odds, unless the Lord was helping her?

Christians must lift their voices with the prophets and boldly declare: "Hear the word of the Lord, O nations, and declare it in the isles afar off, and say, 'He who scattered Israel will gather him, and keep him as a shepherd does his flock.'"[6]

The Voice of Jesus and the Apostles

For Christians, it is certainly important to know what Jesus said about the future of Israel and Jerusalem. Jesus said, "And they will fall by the edge of the sword and be led away captive into all nations. And Jerusalem will be trampled by Gentiles, until the times of the Gentiles are fulfilled."[7]

In this statement, Jesus made four major predictions about the future of Jerusalem. First, He predicted the destruction of Jerusalem. His prediction came true when the Romans destroyed the city in A.D. 70.

Second, Jesus said His Jewish brethren would be dispersed among the nations. This also came true. The Romans scattered the Jews where they have lived among the nations. But the cry of their heart has always been, "Next year in Jerusalem." Third, Jesus said the Gentile nations would dominate Jerusalem, as they have for the past 2,000 years.

But Jesus also spoke of a distant time when Gentile domination of Jerusalem would come to an end and the Jews would once again control their ancient city. This prophecy of Jesus was fulfilled in 1967 when Israel took control of biblical Jerusalem. For the first time in 2,000 years, Jerusalem came under the sovereignty of the Jewish people.

The predictions Jesus made about Jerusalem have certainly come true. Shouldn't Christians believe the dramatic liberation of Jerusalem to be the fulfillment of His words? Since Jesus said it is God's plan to end Gentile rule of Jerusalem, shouldn't Christians support Israel in her efforts to keep Jerusalem as her undivided capital?

In addition to His prophecies, Jesus instructed His followers to assist His Jewish kinsman during their times of distress. Repeating an earlier quotation, Jesus said:

> *Come you blessed of My Father, inherit the kingdom prepared for you from the foundation of the world: for I was hungry and you gave Me food; I was thirsty and you gave Me drink; I was a stranger and you took Me in; I was naked and you clothed Me; I was sick and you visited Me; I was in prison and you came to Me. Then the righteous will answer Him saying, "Lord, when did we see You hungry and feed You, or thirsty and give You drink? When did we see You a stranger and take You in, or naked and clothe You? Or when did we see You sick or in prison, and come to You?" And the King will answer and say to them, "Assuredly, I say to you, inasmuch as you did it to one of the least of these My brethren, you did it to Me."*[8]

The apostle Paul also spoke about Christians helping Jews in their time of need. He wrote, "It pleased them [the Christians] indeed, and they are their [the Jews] debtors. For if the Gentiles have been partakers of their spiritual things, their duty is also to minister to them in material things."[9]

While six million Jews perished in the Holocaust, the Christian world hardly raised its voice. Only a few courageous believers were faithful to our Lord's words. Where were the Christians when the Jews needed us? We must not repeat our failures of the past. We want a peaceful solution to the Arab-Israeli conflict. We want justice and compassion for all sides. We don't always agree how this should best be accomplished, but we must support Israel in her time of need!

The Voice of History

It is often said that the key to the future lies in the past. What would the historical voice say about the current Arab-Israeli conflict?

While we are not certain of the exact dates Jews settled in Israel, King David established Jerusalem as the capital of Israel around 1000 B.C. This means that Israel, with Jerusalem as her capital, existed almost 1,000 years before the beginning of Christianity and 1,600 years before the rise of Islam.

In A.D. 135, the Roman Emperor Hadrian renamed Israel. He gave it the name of the ancient enemy of the Jews, the Philistines. He called it—Palestine! The land was known by this name until the rebirth of the State of Israel in 1948. So it was the Jews, not the Palestinians, who lived in the land. While God called the land, Israel, the world called it Palestine.

Throughout history, Israel was ruled by many empires. However, it is important to understand that none of these empires ever established a sovereign state in the land and Jerusalem has never been the capital of any country since the time of King David.

Because of severe persecution, Russian Jews began immigrating to Israel in the 1880s. A second wave of immigration, also from Russia, was in 1905. This was followed by later immigrations resulting in a growing Jewish population in Israel.

As we learned in an earlier chapter, the Jewish pioneers did not steal the land from Arabs. They settled on land that was unoccupied, deserted, or purchased. The Jews own the land, if for no other reason, because they bought it.

As the Jews worked the land of Israel, it began to prosper. While both Jews and Arabs lived in pre-Israel Palestine, there were many poor migrant Arab farm workers who lived in the neighboring countries and needed work. When the Arabs heard that the land was prospering, hundreds of thousands of them migrated to Israel to benefit. Many of the Palestinian Arabs today are the descendants of these same migrant workers from Israel's neighboring countries. Over time, the population of this group of Arabs increased.

We certainly understand the needs of Palestinian Arabs. Those who want to live in peace with Israel should have that opportunity. But they simply do not have a valid historical claim and bonding to the land as do the Jews.

In spite of what many assume to be true, there has never been a sovereign land called Palestine. Jerusalem has never been a Palestinian capital. As a matter of fact, Arab leaders themselves denied the existence of an Arab country called Palestine. It simply did not exist.

We earlier quoted Professor Phillip Hitti, a very distinguished Princeton professor and Arab historian. He said in a speech in 1946, "There is no such thing as Palestine in Arab history, absolutely not."[10]

When foreign powers ruled the land, Israel was just a "province" of their empire. These rulers never established a sovereign state in the land, and Jerusalem was never a capital of any country other than the Jews.

The Voice of International Recognition

British foreign minister, James Balfour believed that England had a responsibility to assist the Jews in establishing their home in Israel in payment of Christianity's great debt to the Jewish people. In 1917, he issued the famous "Balfour Declaration" acknowledging the national rights of the Jews to a homeland in Israel.

The Foreign Minister sent the following letter to Lord Rothschild:

> Dear Lord Rothschild, I have much pleasure in conveying to you, on behalf of his Majesty's Government, the following declaration of sympathy with the Jewish Zionist aspirations which has been submitted to, and approved by, the cabinet.
>
> "His Majesty's Government view with favor the establishment in Palestine of a national home for the Jewish people, and will use their best endeavors to facilitate the achievement of this object, it being clearly understood that nothing shall be done which may prejudice the civil and religious rights of existing non-Jewish communities in Palestine, or the rights and political status enjoyed by Jews in an other country."
>
> I should be grateful if you would bring this declaration to the knowledge of the Zionist Federation.[11]

At the San-Remo Conference held on April 25, 1920, the newly formed League of Nations assigned Britain the mandate to administer Israel. This allowed for the practical implementation of the Balfour Declaration.

Before World War I, the region called "Greater Syria" included what is now Jordan, Lebanon, Israel and Syria. The Ottoman Turkish empire ruled over this area from 1517-1917. At the end of the war, the British and French divided the territory into the above mentioned states under the oversight of the League of Nations. The French took control of Syria and Lebanon while Britain was given the mandate to govern the area of Palestine, which later became Israel and Jordan.

The British had also made promises to the Arabs in the region. In exchange for assistance in fighting against the Turks, the British had appointed Ibn Ali Hussein as the Sherif (ruler) of Mecca and made him vague nationalistic promises. But the British has also made promises to the French and the Zionists. The British had promised Hussein that his son, Faisal would be king of the newly created state of Syria. But when the French took over Syria, the British created modern Iraq (1921) and made Faisal king of Iraq.

To further placate Hussein, then British Colonial Secretary Winston Churchill, in 1922, took the land east of the Jordan River that was promised to the Zionists and created a new state they called Transjordan (across the Jordan). This was approximately 77 percent of the land promised to the Jews. The British then appointed Abdullah, another son of Sherif Hussein, the King of Transjordan. The British made Transjordan an Arab Palestinian state, while Palestine, later Israel, was to be the Jewish Palestinian state.

Meanwhile, Sheriff Hussein was defeated by Ibn Saud in 1925 and exiled to Cyprus where he died in 1931. Saud became the ruler of Saudi Arabia and made it an independent kingdom in 1926. Lebanon and Syria gained independence from France in 1943 and 1946 respectively. Transjordan was granted independence in 1946 and renamed Jordan. Israel became a state on May 14, 1948.

In 1919, Faisal met with the Zionist leader Chaim Weizmann and agreed to the establishment of a Jewish state in Palestine as long as the British kept their promise to grant the Arabs independence. Today, there are 22 Arab independent states. Yet, they still do not recognize the legitimate right of Israel to exist as a sovereign state in their midst.

During World War II, Britain greatly curtailed Jewish immigration to Israel even while Jews were desperately seeking to escape Nazi Germany. For example, in 1939, Britain issued a decree which established a quota limiting Jewish immigration to 10,000 refugees for each of the next five years, plus another 25,000 refugees. At the end of this period, no further Jewish immigration would be permitted without Arab consent.

On April 29, 1947, the newly formed United Nations approved a resolution to partition the land between the Jews and the Arabs. The Jews reluctantly accepted the partition which gave them much less than originally promised in the Balfour Declaration. The Arabs rejected the resolution. On May 14, 1948, 30 years of British rule and the mandate of Israel ended.

The Western powers, particularly Britain, artificially created the modern Arab states. Britain made promises to all of them which they could not keep. Conflict of interests in the region as well as inter-Arab hostilities and Zionists aspirations form the background for the current problems in the Middle East. While there has been much turmoil, the voice of international recognition spoke on behalf of the rights of the Jewish people to their ancient homeland.

The Voice of Humanitarianism

Throughout history Jews have been severely persecuted while living under Christian and Moslem rule. Under Islamic rule, beginning with the Omar Charter, both Jews and Christians suffered much persecution and humiliation, the intensity of which was determined by the character of the particular Moslem ruler. Christians and Jews were considered second-class citizens who were forced to submit to Islamic superiority.

Unfortunately, Christian nations have been less tolerant of Jews than were the Moslems. They also viewed the Jews as second-class citizens who were forever to be marked and branded as outcasts from the normal order and decencies of society. Christian anti-Semitism culminated in the Crusades, the Inquisition, Russian Pograms, and the Holocaust. Most people are not aware that Hitler took some of his ideas for the "final solution" from Christian theology and practice.

After 2,000 years of persecution and discrimination, caused in part by false Christian teaching blaming the Jews for the death of Jesus, shouldn't we Christians repent of our anti-Semitism and the suffering we have inflicted on the Jews? Don't we have a responsibility to the people who gave us our Bible and our Savior? Shouldn't we raise our voice with them and say, "Never Again!"

Israel assimilated 800,000 Jewish refugees from the Arab countries when the new State of Israel was born. These people, modern Israelis, were forced to leave their homes and flee for their lives by Arab regimes that persecuted them and confiscated their possessions. In more recent times, Israel has absorbed over a million Jews from the former Soviet Union.

Yet, in the midst of their hardships and suffering, the Lord promises His blessing on those returning to the land, "For the Lord will comfort Zion, He will comfort all her waste places; He will make her wilderness like Eden, and her desert like the garden of the Lord; joy and gladness will be found in it, thanksgiving and the voice of melody."[12]

Personal Study Review

1. What does the voice of Scripture and the prophets say about the Arab-Israeli conflict?

2. What does the voice of Jesus and the apostles say about the Arab-Israeli conflict?
3. What does the voice of history say?
4. What does the voice of international recognition say?
5. What does the voice of humanitarianism say?

Chapter 12

CHRISTIANS AND THE ARAB-ISRAELI CONFLICT PART 2

The voices we have just heard are loud and clear regarding the rightful ownership of the land of Israel to the Jewish people. It shouldn't be difficult to understand that the God of the Bible promised the land of the Bible to the people of the Bible, that is the Jewish people. However, it seems that some people are just hard of hearing. So in this chapter, we will listen to more voices that speak clearly about this conflict.

THE VOICE OF MORALITY

There are moral reasons for Christians supporting Israel. Consider the overwhelming size of the Arab countries compared to Israel. There are over 20 countries in the Arab League of states with a population of over 200 million. The population of Israel is approximately 6 million. The territories of the Arab League states are more than 500 times the size of Israel. They are more than a third larger than Europe and more than 50 percent larger than the United States. Israel is about the size of the State of New Jersey in the U.S.

If Israel were to lose a war with her Arab neighbors, she would cease to exist. The Jewish people would no longer have a homeland. This would invalidate all the places in the Bible where God promises to give the land to the Jewish people. This would mean that the Bible is a lie and that the God of Bible is not the one true God.

For Jews, it would mean that Abraham, Isaac, Jacob, Moses, King David and all the prophets were wrong. For Christians, it would mean that the New Testament and the life and teachings of Jesus are a lie. In other words, Jews and Christians are worshipping a false God and should convert to Islam. For this, and many other reasons, Christians must support Israel in her quest to live in the land given to her by the Almighty. We have a moral and a theological imperative.

Both Judaism and Christianity place great emphasis on the worth of the individual, personal liberty, and equality. History has shown that these values are best encouraged through democratic forms of government, not totalitarian regimes. Democracies rarely go to war with each other because their leaders are accountable to their citizens for the blood shed by their sons and daughters. For this reason, democracies promote peace and stability in the world.

In order to function effectively, democratic forms of government must have a clear separation of powers with organizational entities that guarantee human rights with a free and independent press, free markets, freedom of speech, freedom of worship, and other personal liberties.

Israel is a young country still learning how to administer a government that is responsive to the needs of all of her citizens. There are many challenges ahead. Yet, Israel is the only democracy in the

Middle East. As such, Israel shares our Christian values of life, liberty, justice, and equality.

Jesus said, "Let your light so shine before men, that they may see your good works and glorify your Father in Heaven."[1] Don't Christians have a moral obligation to help Israel shine the light of democracy and freedom in a Middle East still living in the darkness of totalitarianism?

Unfortunately, Israel's Arab neighbors do not share our Judeo-Christian values regarding human rights. Their political systems are totalitarian by nature. There is no real legitimate political opposition to the various Arab regimes. Those who criticize government policies are considered traitors. State control of the press keeps the citizenry in darkness with distorted views of history and world events.

In the Arab press, Israel is constantly presented as the villain that must be destroyed. Children are taught to hate Jews and to pursue glorious martyrdom fighting them. Those who advocate human rights, freedom of speech, and a free press are intimidated or murdered. This includes Christians as well as Arabs.

While it is not widely known, millions of Christians live in Middle Eastern countries. They too are suffering horrible atrocities under totalitarian regimes. For example, in Sudan, entire villages are being destroyed. Men are crucified, the women are raped, and children are taken from their families and made slaves. The Arab-Israeli conflict is not the only one in the Middle East. Shouldn't Christians raise the voice of morality and human rights on behalf of our persecuted brothers and sisters?

Some Christians say they don't have problems with Jews, but they do have problems with Israel. Perhaps it is helpful to be reminded that Israel is basically a "Jewish" state. We Christians should voice our legitimate concerns, but we must give moral support to the only state in the Middle East that shares our values. That state is Israel.

THE VOICE OF THE LAND

The Lord said that the Promised Land was a land flowing with milk and honey (Exodus 3:8). Yet, for many centuries, the land was desolate. It seemed that the Almighty had forgotten His promise to bless the land.

When we study the history of the land, we see it only prospers when the Jews are living in it. After the Romans expelled the Jews from Israel in the first and second centuries of this era, the land progressively deteriorated. Since there was never a sovereign state in the land, nor was it the capital of any empire, Israel became a neglected wasteland.

The condition of the land further deteriorated when it was part of the Turkish Empire (1517-1917). With no concern for the land, the Turks exploited what they could from it, even to the point of placing a tax on the trees. The people living in the land were very poor. They certainly could not afford to pay taxes on trees, so they cut them down.

Land cannot produce without trees. A land without trees that had been overgrazed and neglected with no conservation soon lost its topsoil. The population of Israel was further reduced, as the people found it almost impossible to live off the land.

When Mark Twain visited Israel in 1867, he wrote "it was a land that sat in sackcloth and ashes, desolate and unlovely."[2] The voice of the land was crying out for its rightful owners to return and once again make it a land of milk and honey.

Since the Jews returned to the land in the 1880s they reclaimed it by planting millions of trees, draining the swamps, establishing agricultural communities, building irrigation works, etc. Israel has found ways to make the desert bloom. She raises fish in the desert, ships flowers to the Netherlands, and exports food to her neighbors.

Israel is a modern miracle. In addition to reclaiming the land, Israel has built a thriving economy, modern systems of transportation, and created industries and jobs for her citizens. Israel has many outstanding achievements in science, agriculture, health care, industry and technology, education, culture and the arts. These achievements could bless all of the Middle East if there was peace.

As just one example, Ben-Gurion University of the Negev, as well as Hebrew University and others in Israel, have pioneered important biotechnology for agricultural development in semi-desert regions. This will help in food production in areas that would not normally be fruitful. Also, drip irrigation methods developed in Israel help conserve scarce water resources.

With all of its problems, Israel is once again a land flowing with milk and honey. This is because of the blood, sweat, and tears of the Jewish pioneers who have reclaimed it. The younger generation of Israelis would do well to remember the great sacrifices their grandparents paid so they could enjoy the blessings of living in the land of Israel.

The Voice of Christian Holy Sites

We often hear voices say that Jerusalem must be made an international city in order to protect the holy sites and guarantee Christian worshipers freedom of access. Christians already have free access to our holy sites, as well as do Muslims and people of every other religion. The government of Israel and the people of Israel are fully committed to freedom of religion and free access for all religious groups to their holy sites. Worshipers of any religion can freely go to their religious shrines or holy sites.

In 1967, when Israel captured the Old City of Jerusalem, the Israeli government established a policy to safeguard free access to holy sites. The Protection of Holy Places Law reads, "The Holy Places shall be protected from desecration and any other violation and from anything likely to violate the freedom of access of members of the various religions to the places sacred to them, or their feelings with regard to those places."[3]

Those of us who have taken Christian tour groups to Israel for many years have always had free access to sites holy to Christians. Israel is protecting these sites for us. Unfortunately, the Palestine intifada can cause security problems to a degree that it may become necessary to temporarily close a holy site for safety purposes.

It must be pointed out that this is in stark contrast to the time when East Jerusalem and Christian holy sites were under Jordanian rule from 1948-1967. King Hussein was considered the most moderate Moslem leader. In spite of his assurances to respect Christians and Christian sites and shrines, Jordan issued decrees severely limiting Christian worship.

Christian schools were required to close on Friday (the Muslim holy day), and Christian students were forced to learn the Koran taught by Muslim teachers. Christian institutions were forbidden to acquire additional property, and Mosques were built next to Christian churches to prevent the expansion of church facilities. Christian access to holy sites was severely limited. Eliyah Tal describes the total deterioration of the Old City of Jerusalem under Jordanian administration from 1948-1967.[4]

Things were worse for the Jews. Jordan made a systematic attempt to eliminate the Jewish presence from Jerusalem. The superior Jordanian military forced the Jewish residents of the Old City to evacuate and forbade them to reenter the Jordanian controlled part of the city. The Old City was transformed into an armed camp.

With no one to restrain them, Jordan destroyed all 58 synagogues in the Old City of Jerusalem and desecrated the Jewish cemetery on the Mount of Olives. They ripped thousands of Jewish gravestones out of the ground and used them to build the walls, pavements, and latrines of Jordanian army camps.[5]

Yasser Arafat, and those who have succeeded him, claim that they will raise the Palestinian flag over every church and synagogue in Jerusalem. This is not just rhetoric. Given the chance, they mean to do what they say. What do you think they would do if they had control of Christian holy sites? Considering their history and their recent violence, Christian holy sites will not be safe under the control of the Palestinian Authority, Hamas or any other terrorist group. They would destroy them or, at best, use them as a means to make money to further their terrorist activities.

The Voice of Jerusalem

Jerusalem is the symbol that stands at the center of the conflict between the Arabs and the Jews. It represents the heart and soul of the struggle. In their zeal for Jerusalem, both Jews and Muslims claim the Holy City as their own.

The Jews claim a historical and spiritual bond to the land that is so strong the Bible says that they are married to the land (Isaiah 62:4-5). The Palestinian Arabs claim they have been in the land from time immemorial but were dispossessed by the Jews. What does the voice of Jerusalem say regarding her rightful owners?

The Jews have a documented history of living in Jerusalem for 3,000 years. They have had a continuous presence in Jerusalem, except for brief periods of forced exile throughout history when Jerusalem was under foreign rule. The Jews have comprised the largest single community in the Old City of Jerusalem from 1820 to our present time. Eliyahu Tal provides the following statistics[6]:

JEWISH MAJORITY IN JERUSALEM

	Jews	**Moslems**	**Christians**
1838	6,000	5,000	3,000
1876	12,000	7,560	5,470
1909	45,000	12,000	10,200
1948	99,320	36,680	31,300
1990	353,200	124,200	14,000

You can tell how important something is to people by how often they speak of it. We should get a good idea how important Jerusalem is to Jews and Muslims by reading their holy books, the Hebrew Bible for the Jews and the Koran for the Arab Muslims. What do their voices say?

Jerusalem is mentioned over 800 times in the Bible. There are 657 references in the Hebrew Bible and 154 references in the New Testament. Yet, Jerusalem is not mentioned even once in the Koran. There is no reason it should be because Mohammed never went to Jerusalem. It is interesting to note that observant Jews pray facing Jerusalem while Muslims pray facing Mecca. Jews make pilgrimages to Jerusalem. Muslims make pilgrimages to Mecca.

Historically, Jerusalem has not been of major importance to Islam. The idea that the Temple Mount is the "third holiest site of

Islam" is a recent development. As explained in Chapter Six, Islamic tradition teaches the myth that Mohammed made a night flight to a mosque on the Temple Mount. However, Mohammed died decades before a mosque was built on the Temple Mount.

Mohammed died in A.D. 632, six years before Jerusalem fell to the Arabs under Caliph Omar in 638. The Dome of the Rock was not built until 692, which is 60 years after Mohammed's death. The Al-Aqsa Mosque was not built until 712, which is 80 years after Mohammed's death.

Even in modern times, the Muslim attitude toward Jerusalem has been one of indifference. When Jordan controlled East Jerusalem and the Temple Mount from 1948-1967, they did not think Jerusalem important enough to make it a Palestinian or Arab capital. It was only when the Jews regained control of the Temple Mount that we learn it was the "third holiest site in Islam."

As I have previously explained, Muslims today claim that the Hebrew Scriptures (Old Testament) is not a valid historical document with respect to the Jewish presence in the land of Israel. They also deny any evidence of a Jewish Temple on the Temple Mount. Christians should speak out against these obvious distortions.

The Voice of America's National Interest

As an American, I am grateful to God for the many blessings He has given my country. I believe one of the reasons God has blessed America is because we have blessed the Jews and stood firm in our support for Israel.

A strong, secure Israel is in the national interest of the United States politically, militarily, economically, socially, and spiritually. Let us consider the following.

Israel is the only true democratic state in the Middle East. As such, Israel shares our values of representative government.

Israel's neighbors are authoritative regimes dictating government policies with little accountability to their citizens. They are repressive and do not allow for human rights. They rule by force rather than the will of the people. Because dictatorships are not servants to the people, their citizens suffer and struggle to survive on the most basic of human necessities.

In order to stay in power, dictators must have an outside enemy to blame for their citizens suffering and poor living conditions. To the Arab world, that outside enemy is Israel. Israel becomes the common enemy who must be eliminated. Arab leaders fear democracy because it would make them accountable to the people. Instead of being a government of the people, for the people, and by the people, Arab dictators prefer to continue their hostilities against Israel.

Israel is an important military ally as a front line defense against radical Islamic fundamentalism. As we know, countries such as Iraq and Iran view America as "The Great Satan" and enemy of Islam. Their leaders continually call for a "holy war" against us. The President of Iran imagines what the world would be like without Israel and America.

These countries seem a long way off from America. Yet, they are developing weapons of mass destruction that, in the very near future, will be able to reach our shores. Furthermore, radical Islamic cells have been established throughout America and are waiting for the right moment to terrorize us.

Israel's military strength is important for our national security. When Iraq built a nuclear reactor with the potential of making nuclear bombs, Israel dispatched F15 and F16 fighter planes and destroyed it on June 7, 1981.

On August 2, 1990, Iraq invaded Kuwait. The United States established a massive military force in Saudi Arabia and the Persian Gulf which was soon joined by a coalition of forces from other countries. On January 17, 1991, U.S. led forces attacked Iraq for the purpose of liberating Kuwait. How many of our American sons and daughters would have died in Operation Desert Storm if Israel had not earlier destroyed Iraq's nuclear capabilities?

The United States economy depends on a steady supply of oil at stable prices. When Iraq invaded Kuwait, the price of oil jumped from $17 to $30 a barrel. The economy of every nation was affected. Furthermore, if Iraq had been successful, Saddam Hussein would have been in control of 20 percent of the world's oil supplies. Our continued prosperity and way of life would be threatened. The second invasion of Iraq under President George W. Bush triggered a huge spike in oil prices that all Americans feel "at the pump."

A strong, secure Israel discourages violent Arab aggression, which contributes to stability in the region and economic strength for America. It is in our own self-interest to have a strong Israel, as this ensures peace in the region.

Israel is important to America socially because she shares our values of human rights, tolerance, freedom, and the sanctity of life. While Israel protects her children, Islamic terrorists send their children to fight their battles, knowing that the whole world will watch as the television cameras show Israeli soldiers firing at them. It is tragic that Yasser Arafat and his terrorist associates have successfully passed their hate for Israel to the next generation. In the natural course of events, it will take generations, if ever, to re-educate these young people to agree to live in peace with Israel.

Finally, Israel is important to America spiritually because we share a Judeo-Christian ethic. The biblical truths of accountability to our Creator, the dignity of mankind, and the importance of moral character and service to others has been the foundation of

Western culture that has made America great. Christians must stand with Israel because we are bound together through a common spiritual heritage.

THE VOICE OF HAYM SALOMON

In 1975 the United States Postal Department issued a commemorative stamp honoring a Jewish man named Haym Salomon for his contribution to the seemingly lost cause of the American Revolution. This unusual stamp was printed on the front and back. On the glue side of the stamp, the following words were printed:

"Financial hero, businessman and broker, Haym Salomon was responsible for raising most of the money needed to finance the American Revolution and later to save the new nation from collapse."

Historians who have studied the story of Haym Salomon all agree that without his "contribution to the cause" there would be no America today. Who was Haym Salomon? Why does America owe him a debt? And why don't we learn about him in school?

The following information about Haym Salomon is readily available on the Internet for anyone who wants to do their own research. I first learned his story from my dear friend, David Allen Lewis, who told the story years ago at a gathering in Washington, DC. I am indebted to David for his excellent research and for sharing what he learned. The following information is a combination of what I have learned from my own research as well as from David's excellent publication, *Israel and the USA: Restoring the Lost Pages of American History*.

Haym Salomon was a successful, financial broker who bought and sold financial paper to raise money for Robert Morris and the Continental Congress. At that time, the Continental Congress had no power to tax the Colonists. They could not raise money for Washington's troops. The war effort was continually on the brink of disaster.

The revolutionary fighters were barely surviving against the superior British forces. They were a pitiful sight fighting on courage alone. It looked as if defeat was certain. When Haym Salomon saw the condition of Washington's troops, he was shocked.

Haym Salomon was a Polish Jew and son of a rabbi from the "Old Country." He was an authentic American patriot and "Son of the Republic." He believed that America would be a safe haven for the Jews. But he also believed that one day in the future, Jerusalem would rise from the dust and the Jews would return to their ancient homeland. Haym believed that Israel and Jerusalem would once again be the home of the wandering Jew.

Salomon determined to do all that he could to help finance the American Revolution so that America could survive until that future time when his people would once again fill the streets of Jerusalem. Historians who have studied the story of this American patriot agree that without the money he gave and raised, there would be no United States of America.

The following Congressional record dated March 25, 1975 tells the story of the financial assistance Salomon gave to Robert Morris[7]:

> When Morris was appointed Superintendent of Finance, he turned to Salomon for help in raising the money needed to carry on the war and later to save the emerging nation from financial collapse. Salomon not only advanced direct loans to the government, he also gave generously of his own resources to pay the salaries of government officials and army officers. With frequent entries of "I sent for Haym Salomon," Morris' diary for the years 1781-1784 records seventy-five transactions between the two men.

David Lewis tells of one last appeal by Robert Morris. He writes, "After the war was over, and George Washington became President of the United States of America, it seemed that disaster loomed on each horizon. Robert Morris appealed to Haym Salomon one last time for aid. But this time Salomon was laying on his deathbed in his home in Philadelphia. Salomon could not refuse. Though dying of tuberculosis, he dragged his pain racked body out of bed, left his home, and went to the coffeehouse where he opened his brokerage operation one last time...."[8]

Haym Salomon was able to raise the money needed to save the fledging new nation from disastrous bankruptcy. We read the following record in the Encyclopedia Britannic:

> Among his many contributions to the Colonies, Haym Salomon subscribed heavily to needed government loans, endorsed notes, gave generously to soldiers, and equipped several military units with his own money. Robert Morris records in his diary that between 1781 and 1784 Salomon lent more than $200,000. In addition he made private loans to prominent statesmen such as James Madison, Thomas Jefferson, and James Monroe, from which he would not take interest. In all, the government owed Salomon more than $600,000. Generations of his descendants tried in vain to collect some portion of these loans, which help to impoverish Salomon in the last years of his life.[9]

Having given his fortune to the cause and with failing health, Haym Salomon died sick and penniless at the age of 45, January 6, 1785. He left behind a young widow, Rachel, and four children all under the age of seven. There were no provisions left for them as Salomon gave his entire fortune for the Revolution.

David Lewis reports:

> Rachel tried for months after Haym's death to collect on personal loans that he had made to Robert Morris,

> to the Congress and others. She was requested to turn all her securities and certificates over to the State Treasurer of Pennsylvania for evaluation. After several months she made further inquiries and was informed that all of the papers relating to her inheritance had been lost.[10]

Haym Salomon is buried in Philadelphia in the Mikveh Israel Cemetery in a grave which is now unmarked. Since we don't know which grave is his, we cannot even pay our respect at his graveside, nor erect a marker. In 1917, a descendant, William Salomon placed a plaque on the brick wall at the cemetery honoring his ancestor. Was it just a coincidence or divine providence that this was the year the British government issued the Balfour Declaration recognizing the rights of the Jewish people to their ancient homeland?

As citizens of America, we can never repay the great debt we owe to this American patriot. But as he stood by our country in its struggles to survive, we can honor him by standing firm in our support and prayers for a safe Israel and a united Jerusalem under the care of Haym Salomon's spiritual descendants, the Jewish people. Christians and Jews must be say with resolve, "For Zion's sake I will not hold My peace, and for Jerusalem's sake I will not rest, until her righteousness goes forth as brightness, and her salvation as a lamp that burns."[11]

The United Nations Record on Israel

The Bible and history give a clear record of the will of God regarding Israel. Yet, of the 175 UN Security Council resolutions passed before 1990, 97 of these resolutions were directed against Israel. Of the 690 General Assemble resolutions voted on before 1990, 429 were directed against Israel.

Former American President Bill Clinton joined with the United Nations is calling for the division of the land and Jerusalem.

President George W. Bush has also called for the division of the land. The U.S. State Department has not recognized Israel's sovereign rights to Jerusalem as her undivided capital.

The God of Abraham, Isaac, and Jacob is a faithful, covenant-keeping God. He will bless Israel in spite of her problems because the time to favor Zion has come. Israel will eventually dwell in a peaceful habitation, in secure dwellings, and in quiet places. Jerusalem shall be inhabited as a town without walls for the Lord Himself will be a wall of fire around her, and His glory will be in her midst (Zechariah 2:4-5).

The prophet Micah explained: "'In that day,' says the Lord, 'I will assemble the lame, I will gather the outcast and those whom I have afflicted; I will make the lame a remnant, and the outcast a strong nation; so the Lord will reign over them in Mount Zion from no on, even forever.'"[12]

While God will bless those who bless Israel, He will surely judge those who oppose His will. As we learn from the Bible:

> *For behold in those days and at that time, when I bring back the captives of Judah and Jerusalem, I will also gather all nations, and bring them down to the Valley of Jehoshaphat; and will enter into judgment with them there on account of My people, My heritage Israel, whom they have scattered among the nations; they have also divided up My land.*[13]

Personal Study Review

1. What does the voice of morality say about the Arab-Israeli conflict?
2. What does the voice of the land say about the Arab-Israeli conflict?

3. What does the voice of Christian holy sites say about the conflict?
4. What does the voice of Jerusalem say about the conflict?
5. What does the voice of America's national interest say about the conflict?
6. What does the voice of Haym Salomon say about the conflict?

Chapter 13

CHRISTIANS AND ISRAEL

Christians and Jews alike spend years studying prophecies in the Bible that talk about the end of the age and the coming of the Messiah. In times past, these prophecies seemed to be about events in the far distant future. All of this changed in 1948 when Israel became a state. Bible believers no longer have to be content just reading about Bible prophecy, we can now be part of it.

When Christians discover this exciting reality, they want to get involved but often don't know what they can do or how to participate with the Lord in His end-time work. While there are many ways to partner with God in this last great work of redemption, the following "action points for Israel" provide helpful guidelines. These guidelines provide practical ways for Christian believers to come along side Israel and the Jewish people in the *Diaspora*.

It is not enough for Christians to study the Scriptures and be knowledgeable about what God is doing in our times prophetically.

It is not enough to attend conferences and seminars and talk about these things to our friends. It is not enough just to lead a Bible study. It is not enough to go to an "Israel friendly" church or congregation. It is not enough to learn the "Songs of Zion" and Israeli dances.

We must also act on what we know. Faith without works of covenantal love is not true biblical faith. We must partner with God to move forward His plan of redemption for Israel and the nations. We are most privileged to be living in these exciting times. But with privilege, comes responsibility.

Christians can partner with God in this exciting work to build up Zion through the following five action steps. The author has spent over 20 years pioneering these action steps. For further information on how you can put these steps into practice in your own life, contact him at his web address given in the back of this book.

ACTION STEP 1: STUDY THE BIBLICAL HEBRAIC ROOTS OF CHRISTIANITY AND ISRAEL IN PROPHECY

Most Christians (and Jews) do not realize there is a vital connection between Christianity and Judaism that was severed by the Christian church centuries ago. Once that severing took place, biblical Judaism and biblical Christianity, which God intended to be one, went their separate ways with tragic consequences for both.

The result of this separation was that the church embraced Greek and Roman concepts and practices and established anti-Semitic policies of hatred and violence toward the Jewish people. This ultimately led to the Holocaust.

While Christians must never forget the past, this is a new day for thousands of believers around the world who are discovering that biblical Christianity has its roots in Jerusalem and biblical Judaism.

The apostle Paul wrote: "Do not boast against the branches [Jews]. But if you do boast, remember that you do not support the root [the Hebraic origins of Christianity] but the root supports you [Christianity]."[1]

We thank God for all of His people who have given their lives in times past to move forward God's redemptive plans and purposes. But it is imperative to realize that the roots of Christianity are not in Athens, Rome, Geneva, Wittenberg, Aldersgate, Azuza Street, Nashville, or Tulsa. They are in Jerusalem, and the Lord is calling believers back to their roots. We must go "back to the future" in order to go forward with God.

You see, there were 2,000 years of Hebrew history, culture, language, traditions and customs that formed the root of Christianity. The more Christians learn the biblical Hebraic-Jewish roots of Christianity, the more fruitful and blessed they can be in their lives.

While Christians in America view life with a Western mind and worldview, the Bible was written by Abraham's descendants who had a Hebraic culture, language, and worldview. American believers have a Middle Eastern book that they seek to understand from their Western culture.

Our Western perspective can easily cause us to misunderstand the Bible. Furthermore, our mind has been more influenced by Greek philosophy than biblical, Hebraic thought. We need a paradigm shift in our thinking regarding theology, history, and the prophetic Scriptures. This is why we must study the biblical Hebraic roots of Christianity.

When we read the Bible through the eyes of its Middle Eastern culture our understanding becomes much richer, deeper, and clearer with more detail than we could ever imagine. We see truths that we are unable to see with our Western eyes, no matter how pure our motives and intense our desires.

Jesus and His early followers were deeply rooted in the rich Hebraic soil of their ancestors. They thought, taught, and lived out of this soil. God planted Christianity in this soil, and we must return to it in order to be biblically nourished.

When Christians are educated in the Jewish roots of their faith, they will understand the great debt Christianity owes to the Jewish people. Their minds will be renewed to think and act biblically. They will understand the prophetic Scriptures concerning Israel. They will want to bless, comfort, love, and support the Jewish people and the people of Israel as commanded in the Bible.

Christians no longer have to be content just reading about prophecy. They will understand prophecy and realize they can become part of its fulfillment. Christians must learn what God is doing in restoring Christianity to its roots, His blessings on the people of Israel and find ways to participate.

The author is a pioneer and spiritual father to many in teaching on the biblical roots of Christianity and the role of Israel in Bible prophecy. If you would like to know how you can learn in the comforts of your own home, contact him for further information.

ACTION POINT 2: ESTABLISH RELATIONSHIPS WITH THE JEWISH COMMUNITY

It is important that Christians reach out to the Jewish community with unconditional love, understanding, and mutual respect.

For too long, Christians, particularly evangelical believers, have only viewed Jews as prospects to convert to Christianity. We have not reached out to the Jewish people with the pure love of God simply because it is the right thing to do as people of God. We have had an attitude of triumphant pride and arrogance that must be replaced with one of humble gratitude and service to the Jewish people.

The Lord Himself commanded us to make disciples of all the nations.[2] Yet, as we share what the Lord has done in our lives, we must love people unconditionally whether they ever acknowledge Jesus as their Messiah, Lord, and Savior. It is God's business to awaken people to their spiritual needs. It is our business as believers to love people unconditionally with a pure heart.

It is has been said that people don't care how much we know until they first know how much we care. How appropriate this statement is for today's Christian-Jewish relationships. People don't need to hear our creeds; they need to see our deeds. As we learn in the New Testament, "My little children let us not love in word or in tongue, but in deed and in truth."[3]

If you are a Christian and have never established relationships with Jewish people, the place to start is with those things you share in common. The two most important concerns Christians and Jews have in common are those related to anti-Semitism and the security of Israel. Christians and Jews around the world are working together through joint conferences, seminars, Holocaust education programs, etc. It is always a challenge for people groups who have been separated for centuries to embrace one another. Yet, the Lord is clearly bringing this about in spite of the barriers and obstacles. If you would like assistance in this important work, contact the author for further information.

GUIDING STATEMENTS FOR JEWISH-CHRISTIAN RELATIONS

The following statements by Jewish and Christian leaders can help guide Christians and Jews as they reach out to one another. The first eight statements were written by leading Jewish and Christian scholars. The Ten Commandments of Christian-Jewish Relationships was written by the author. These statements represent a paradigm shift of monumental significance between Christians and Jews. *The New York Times*, September 10, 2000.[4]

PARADIGM SHIFT BETWEEN JEWS AND CHRISTIANS

1. Jews and Christians worship the same God.
2. Jews and Christians seek authority from the same book—the Bible.
3. Christians can respect the claim of the Jewish people on the Land of Israel.
4. Jews and Christians accept the moral principles of Torah.
5. Nazism was not a Christian phenomenon.
6. The humanly irreconcilable difference between Jews and Christians will not be settled until God redeems the entire world as promised in Scripture.
7. A new relationship between Jews and Christians will not weaken Jewish practice.
8. Jews and Christians must work together for justice and peace.

In response to this ground-breaking statement, I have written what I call, "The Ten Commandments of Christian-Jewish Relationships."

Ten Commandments of Christian-Jewish Relationships

1. The Jews are God's chosen people.
2. God's Covenant with the Jews is eternal.
3. The "Jews" did not kill Christ.
4. The church has not replaced the Jews in God's eternal redemptive purposes.
5. Christians owe a great debt to the Jews.
6. Christians are called to bless and comfort the Jews.
7. Christians share the same Messianic hope with Jews.
8. Christians must stand with the Jews against anti-Semitism.
9. God promised the Jews the Land of Israel with Jerusalem as its eternal, united capital.
10. Christians and Jews have much more in common than differences and, where possible, must work together for righteous causes.

"While we understand that Christians and Jews have theological differences, we do not have to agree on theology in order to love one another. And if we cannot love one another, what good is our theology."[5]

We Christians must repent of our anti-Semitic theology, attitudes, and actions. We must make radical changes in our theology, our thinking, our attitudes, and our priorities. We must understand the prophetic times in which we are living and find ways to relate to the Jewish people "for such a time as this." (Esther 4:14.)

ACTION STEP 3: MAKE A PILGRIMAGE TO ISRAEL AND THE FEAST OF TABERNACLES

One of the best investments a Christian can make in his or her life is to make a pilgrimage to Israel. It is often said that a two-week trip to Israel is worth a year of Bible study. You will not only enrich your own life, but you will be a blessing to the very people God is bringing back to the land, the people of Israel. A trip to Israel will change your life forever.

While it is always a blessing to go to Israel, it is prophesied in the Bible that, in the days of Messiah, people from all the nations will go to Jerusalem to celebrate *Succot*, the Feast of Tabernacles. In fact, the rabbis say that when the nations come to Jerusalem to celebrate *Succot*, it is a sign of the soon coming of Messiah. Christians have the privilege and opportunity, and perhaps responsibility, to fulfill Bible prophecy by making this great pilgrimage.

"And it shall come to pass that everyone who is left of all the nations which came against Jerusalem shall go up from year to year to worship the King, the Lord of hosts, and to keep the Feast of Tabernacles."[6]

"Yes, many peoples and strong nations shall come to seek the Lord of hosts in Jerusalem and to pray before the Lord."[7]

Since 1980, Christians from around the world have made their pilgrimage to Jerusalem to participate in the Christian celebration the Feast of Tabernacles sponsored by the International Christian Embassy of Jerusalem. The author and his wife have had the blessing of leading tours to Israel and the Feast of Tabernacles every year since 1987, where the author has been a featured teacher for many years. They invite you to join them on their next tour. Your life will never be the same.

Action Step 4: Help the Jews make Aliyah

As we have read in previous chapters, the Bible tells us that in the latter years God will bring the Jews back to their ancient land. This promise is repeated many times in the Hebrew Bible. Perhaps the most famous Scripture is the prophecy of the "Valley of Dry Bones" given by the prophet Ezekiel where God said:

> *...Son of man, these bones are the whole house of Israel. They indeed say, Our bones are dry, our hope is lost, and we ourselves are cut off! Therefore prophesy and say to them... "O My people, I will open your graves and cause you to come up from your graves, and bring you into the land of Israel. Then you shall know that I am the Lord, when I have opened your graves, O My people, and brought you up from your graves. I will put My Spirit in you, and you shall live, and I will place you in your own land. Then you shall know that I, the Lord, have spoken it and performed it," says the Lord.*[8]

While many Christians are familiar with this and other related Scriptures, they may not be aware that God calls them to participate in the process of helping the Jews home to Israel. This process is called *Aliyah*, which means to "go up." Christians have a God-given responsibility to help the Jews "go up" to Israel in fulfillment of Bible prophecy.

We have read the following Scriptures in previous chapters but this is a good reminder.

> *...Behold, I will lift My hand in an oath to the nations, and set up My standard for the peoples. They shall bring your sons in their arms, and your daughters shall be carried on their shoulders.*[9]

> *Surely the coastlands shall wait for Me; and the ships of Tarshish will come first, to bring your sons from afar, their silver and their*

> *gold with them, to the name of the Lord your God, and to the Holy One of Israel, because He has glorified you.*[10]

There are a handful of Christian organizations involved in the process of *Aliyah*. Some bring the Jews home by ship, others by air, and still others by land. Over time, Christian organizations have led the way in bringing tens of thousands of Jews to Israel from around the world, but primarily from the Ukraine and the former Soviet Union.

Since God says He will bring all the Jews to Israel from the *Diaspora* (Ezekiel 39:28), many more Christians must be awakened to their responsibilities to partner with God in this great work of redemption. In the future, the *Aliyah* of Jews from the West will take most of our time and resources.

For years, the author and his wife have been actively involved in helping Jews make *Aliyah*. If you would like to know more about how you can participate in this important work, contact them for further information.

ACTION STEP 5:
GIVING SOCIAL ASSISTANCE TO THE IMMIGRANTS

When the Jewish people arrive in Israel, they have very few possessions and little money to buy the most basic necessities of life. They have come to a country where they don't speak the language and don't have a job. They have to study Hebrew, while looking for work and trying to assimilate into Israeli society.

The Israeli government does its best to help the new immigrants. But with over one million new immigrants, and many more coming, they can only offer minimum assistance. This would be a challenge for people with financial means, but it is even more so for people who arrive with little but the clothing on their backs.

Once again, God calls Christians to bless and comfort the Jewish people by providing social assistance to the new immigrants. The prophet Isaiah wrote to the Gentiles: "Comfort, yes, comfort My people!"[11]

Jesus spoke of these times and instructed His followers to assist His Jewish kinsman during their times of distress. We have read the following Scripture several times already. Most Christians are familiar with these words of Jesus. But they may not understand the context. The context is at the end of the age when the Jewish people are being persecuted. The Lord instructs non-Jewish believers to assist the Jews in their distress. God judges us on how we respond.

Jesus said:

> *Come you blessed of My Father, inherit the kingdom prepared for you from the foundation of the world: for I was hungry and you gave Me food; I was thirsty and you gave Me drink; I was a stranger and you took Me in; I was naked and you clothed Me; I was sick and you visited Me; I was in prison and you came to Me. Then the righteous will answer Him saying, "Lord, when did we see you hungry and feed You, or thirsty and give you drink? When did we see You a stranger and take You in, or naked and cloth You? Or when did we see You sick, or in prison, and come to You?" And the King will answer and say to them, "Assuredly, I say to you, inasmuch as you did it to one of the least of these My brethren, you did it to Me.*[12]

The apostle Paul also spoke about Christians helping Jews in their time of need. He wrote, "It pleased them [the Christians] indeed, and they are their [the Jews] debtors. For if the Gentiles have been partakers of their spiritual things, their duty is also to minister to them in material things."[13]

The author and his wife have been involved with Christian organizations in Israel that have been recognized and lauded by the Israeli government for their work in providing social assistance to new immigrants and the poor. If you want to be a personal fulfillment of Bible prophecy by comforting the new immigrants, contact them for further information.

A FINAL WORD

This book was a great challenge to write, and I'm sure it has been a challenge for you to read. While I have had to write some hard things, I have tried to give a word of hope and encouragement along the way to Bible-believing Christians and Jews. While we are living in times of conquest and conflict, the Lord God of Israel is a faithful covenant-keeping God who will fulfill His promises written in the Bible.

In view of this assurance, I want end this book with the prayer King David prayed to the Lord:

> *Blessed are You, Lord God of Israel, our father, forever and ever. Yours, O Lord, is the greatness, the power and the glory, the victory and the majesty; for all that is in heaven and in earth is yours; Yours is the kingdom, O Lord, and you are exalted as head over all. Both riches and honor come from You, and You reign over all. In Your hand is power and might; in Your hand it is to make great and to give strength to all.*[14]

Personal Study Review

1. List and explain the five action points for Israel discussed in this lesson.
2. State your personal thoughts on how you feel God would want you to partner with Him in fulfilling Bible prophecy.

ENDNOTES

CHAPTER 1

1. Richard Booker, *Islam, Christianity and Israel* (Houston: Sounds of the Trumpet, 1994), 3.
2. Robert Morey, *The Islamic Invasion* (Eugene, OR: Harvest Publishers, 1992), 55-56.
3. *Houston Chronicle*, (Houston: September 10, 2006), A14.
4. Ron Peck, *The Shadow of the Crescent* (Springfield, MO: Center for Ministry to Muslims), 18.
5. Abdullah Al-Araby, *The Islamization of America* (Los Angeles: The Pen vs. the Sword, 2003), ix.
6. Ibid., 2.
7. Peck, 1.

8. Ibid.
9. Al-Araby, 1.
10. Ibid., 2.
11. Ibid.
12. Ibid.
13. Ibid.
14. Paul Sperry, *Infiltration*, (Nashville: Nelson Current, a subsidiary of Thomas Nelson, Inc., 2005), XI.
15. Ibid.
16. Ibid., XIII
17. Ibid., XIV-XIX.
18. Peck, 3.
19. Ibid.
20. Ibid., 10-11.
21. Mark Steyn, *America Alone* (Washington, DC: Regnery Publishing, Inc., 2006), 2.
22. Ibid.
23. Ibid.
24. Ibid., xiii
25. Ibid., 3.
26. Peck, 20.

CHAPTER 2

1. John Ankerberg and John Weldon, *The Facts on Islam* (Eugene, OR: Harvest Publishers, 1991), 13-14.

2. Dr. Anis Shorrosh, *Islam Revealed* (Nashville: Thomas Nelson Publisher, 1988), 30-31.
3. Ankerberg and Weldon, 14.
4. Ergun Mehmet Caner and Emir Fethi Caner, *Unveiling Islam* (Grand Rapids, MI: Kregel Publications, 2002), 95-100.
5. Ibid., 96.
6. Ibid., 100.
7. Shorrosh, 29.
8. Ibid., 31.
9. Caner and Caner, 122.
10. Shorrosh, 32.
11. Robert Payne, *The History of Islam* (New York: Barnes and Noble, 1992), 32.
12. Caner and Caner, 125-126.
13. Ibid., 127.
14. Ibid.
15. Shorrosh, 34.
16. Caner and Caner, 128.
17. Caner and Caner, 129.
18. Shorrosh, 34-35.
19. Ibid., 34.
20. Caner and Caner, 162.
21. Ibid., 163.
22. Ibid., 163-164.
23. Ibid., 164.

24. Dore Gold, *Hatred's Kingdom* (Washington, DC: Regnery Publishing, Inc., 2003), 17-29.
25. Ibid.
26. Ibid.
27. Psalm 22:27-28.

CHAPTER 3

1. Morey, *The Moon-god Allah in the Archeology of the Middle East* (Newport, PA: The Research and Education Foundation, 1994), 1-2.
2. Ibid., 3.
3. Ibid., 5.
4. Ibid., 2.
5. Ibid., 3.
6. Ibid., 2.
7. Ibid., 3.
8. Ibid., 5.
9. Ibid., 8.
10. Ibid.
11. Robert Payne, *The History of Islam* (New York: Barnes and Noble, 1992), 4-5
12. Shorrosh, 48.
13. Morey, *Islamic Invasion* (Eugene, OR: Harvest House Publishers, 1992), 71.
14. Shorrosh, 48.
15. Ibid., 49.
16. Ibid., 50.

17. Payne, 13-14.
18. Morey, *By Their Moles Ye Shall Know Them* (Newport, PA: The Research and Education Foundation, 1995).
19. Ibid.
20. Surah, THE CONFEDERATE TRIBES, 36:40.
21. Payne, 14.
22. Morey, *By Their Moles Ye Shall Know Them* (Newport, PA: The Research and Education Foundation, 1995).
23. Ibid.
24. Ibid.
25. Ibid.
26. Ibid.
27. Ibid.
28. Ibid.
29. Ibid.
30. Ibid.
31. Caner and Caner, 41-42.
32. Ibid., 42.
33. Shorrosh, 53.
34. Arthur Jefferey, *Islam: Mohammed and His Religion* (New York: Bobbs-Merrill Company, 1975), 16.
35. Alfred Guillaume, *Islam* (New York: Penguin Books, 1977), 37,56.
36. William Miller, *A Christian's Response to Islam* (Nutley, NJ: Presbyterian and Reformed, 1977), 19-20.
37. Caner and Caner, 42.

38. Shorrosh, 53.
39. Morey, *Islamic Invasion*, 72.
40. Ibid., 78-79.
41. Shorrosh, 56-57.
42. Bernard Lewis, *The Arabs in History* (New York: Harper-Colophon Books, 1966), 31-32.
43. Guillaume, 11-12.
44. Payne, 30-32.
45. Ibid.
46. Shorrosh, 165.
47. Payne, 55-56.
48. Shorrosh, 62.
49. Ibid., 50.
50. Ibid., 71.
51. Caner and Caner, 71-72.
53. Payne, 271-272.
54. Daniel 4:34-35.

CHAPTER 4

1. *Houston Chronicle*, (Houston: February 24, 2007), F4.
2. Surah, CLOTS OF BLOOD, 96:1.
3. Genesis 1:26; 2:7.
4. Deuteronomy 7:7-8.
5. John 3:16.
6. Jeremiah 9:23-24.
7. John 17:3.

8. 1 Chronicles 29:10.
9. Matthew 6:7-9.
10. Exodus 3:13-15.
11. Psalm 29:2.
12. John 17:6,11,26.
13. Isaiah 46:9.
14. Isaiah 44:6-7.
15. 1 Chronicles 17:20-21.
16. Surah, UNBELIEVERS, 109:1-6.
17. Exodus 24:3-4,7-8.
18. 2 Timothy 3:16-17.
19. 2 Peter 1:20-21.
20. Surah, THE COW, 2:90-91.
21. Surah, THE TABLE, 5:13-15.
22. Surah, THE COW, 2:124,127.
23. Surah, BATTLE ARRAY, 6:6.
24. Isaiah 9:6-7.
25. Proverbs 30:4.
26. Psalm 2:7.
27. Matthew 3:17.
28. Surah, ONENESS, 112:1-4.
29. Surah, ORNAMENTS OF GOLD, 43:81.
30. Surah, THE TABLE, 5:72-73.
31. Surah, THE TABLE, 5:75.
32. Surah, THE TABLE, 4:171.

33. Surah, THE NIGHT JOURNEY, 17:111.
34. Surah, WOMEN, 4:157.
35. Surah, THE COW, 2:106.
36. Surah, THE COW, 2:122.
37. Surah, THE TABLE, 5:22.
38. Surah, THE KNEELING, 45:17.
39. Surah, THE COW, 2:62.
40. Surah, THE COW, 2:256.
41. Surah, THE COW, 2:216.
42. Surah, THE COW, 2:190,193.
43. Surah, THE IMRANS, 3:118.
44. Surah, THE IMRANS, 3:150.
45. Surah, THE WOMEN, 4:76.
46. Surah, THE TABLE, 5:33.
47. Surah, THE TABLE, 5:49.
48. Surah, THE TABLE, 5:51.
49. Surah, THE SPOILS, 8:12,59.
50. Surah, REPENTANCE, 9:5.
51. Hadith, Sahih Muslim, Book 041, Number 6985.
52. Canter and Canter, 78.
53. Surah, THE COW, 2:228.
54. Surah, WOMEN, 4:34.
55. Surah, WOMEN, 4:11.
56. Surah, THE COW, 2:282.
57. Surah, IMRANS, 3:14.

58. Surah, WOMEN, 4:3.
59. Surah, THE CONFDERATE TRIBES, 33:59.
60. Surah, THE COW, 2:223.
61. Caner and Caner, 137. Attributed to Mohammed, according to Al Hakim.
62. Surah, THE COW, 2:229.
63. Caner and Caner, 134.
64. Ibid.
65. Surah, PROHIBITION, 66:5.
66. Zechariah 14:9.

CHAPTER 5

1. Genesis 12:1-3.
2. Genesis 16:11-12.
3. Genesis 17:7-9,4.
4. Genesis 1:18-21.
5. Genesis 28:13-15.
6. Genesis 21:20-21.
7. Genesis 25:18.
8. Genesis 28:9.
9. Genesis 36:6,8-9.
10. Genesis 27:40.
11. Genesis 25:6.
12. Ezekiel 35:5-6.
13. Psalm 83:4-5,12.
14. Zechariah 12:8-9.

15. Isaiah 19:24-25.
16. Joel 3:17.
17. Ezekiel 39:21-22,29.
18. Ezekiel 38:23.

CHAPTER 6

1. Joan Peters, *From Time Immemorial* (New York: Harper and Row, 1984), 348.
2. Psalm 122:6.
3. Murray Dixon, *Whose Promised Land?* (Auckland, New Zealand, 1991), 56.
4. Ibid. 29.
5. Peters, 11.
6. Mitchell Bard, *Myths and Facts*, (Chevy Chase, MD: American-Israeli Cooperative Enterprise, 2001) 26.
7. Ibid.
8. Zechariah 12:2-3.
9. Zechariah 12:9.
10. Surah, THE NIGHT JOURNEY, 17:1.
11. Payne, 24-25.
12. Eliyahu Tal, *Whose Jerusalem* (Jerusalem: International Forum for a United Jerusalem, 1994) 65.
13. Surah, THE COW, 2:47.
14. Surah, THE TABLE, 5:22.
15. Zechariah 8:3.

CHAPTER 7

1. Bard, 44-45.
2. Ibid., 162.
3. Peters, 34.
4. Tal, 157-160.
5. Ibid., 154.
6. Ibid., 149.
7. Ibid.
8. Peters, 274.
9. Ibid., 36-363.
10. Bard, 46-49.
11. Ibid.
12. Ibid.
13. Ibid.
14. Ibid.
15. Ibid.
16. Tal, 149-150.
17. Ibid.
18. Zechariah 8:7-8.

CHAPTER 8

1. Psalm 102:12-16.
2. Zechariah 12:2-3,9.
3. Isaiah 34:8.
4. Isaiah 46:9-10,13.

5. Psalm 132:13-14.
6. Psalm 135:21.
7. Psalm 129:5.
8. Ezekiel 38:23.
9. Ezekiel 39:7.
10. Psalm 33:10-12.
11. Psalm 2:1-6.
12. Joel 2:32.
13. Joel 3:16-17.
14. Psalm 22:27-28.
15. Jeremiah 30-11.
16. Ezekiel 11:16-17.
17. Lance Lambert, *Israel: The Unique Land the Unique People* (Wheaton, IL: Tyndale Publishers, 1980), 132. Quoting Amos Elon, Herzl (London, 1975), 16.
18. Ed Vallowe, *The Budding of the Fig Tree* (Forest Park, GA: Ed. F. Vallowe Evangelistic Association, 1972), 37.
19. Malka Drucker, *Eliezer Ben-Yehuda* (New York: Lodestar Books, 1987), 16.

CHAPTER 9

1. 1 Chronicles 11:4-9. (See also 2 Samuel 5:6-9.)
2. 2 Samuel 6:12,17. (See also 1 Chronicles 15-16.)
3. 2 Chronicles 3:1;5:2. (See also 1 Kings 8:1.)
4. 1 Kings 8:10-11. (See also 2 Chronicles 5.)
5. 1 Kings 8:22-23. (See also 2 Chronicles 5.)

6. Ezekiel 10:18-19.
7. Ezekiel 43: 4,7.
8. Isaiah 62:1,6-7.
9. Psalm 122:6-9.
10. Zechariah 8: 2-5,7-9.
11. Walter Laqueur, *A History of Zionism* (New York: Schocken Books, 1972,2003), 80-81.
12. Richard Booker, *The Time to Favor Zion has Come* (Houston: Sounds of the Trumpet, 1996), 26.
13. Ibid., 26-27.
14. Deuteronomy 30:5-6.
15. Romans 11:1,18
16. Genesis 12:1-3.
17. Genesis 12:7.
18. Genesis 13:14-17.
19. Genesis 15:18.
20. Genesis 17:7-8.
21. Genesis 17:18-19.
22. Genesis 28:13-14.
23. 1 Chronicles 16:15-17.
24. Ezekiel 11:16-17.
25. Rabbi Avrohom Chaim Feuer, *Shemoneh Esrei* (Brooklyn, NY: Meshora Publications, 1990, 1995), 153-160.
26. Ibid., 201-210.

27. Isaiah 19:23-25.
28. Amos 9:14-15.

CHAPTER 10

1. Richard Booker, *Jewish Herald Voice* (Houston: 2005), 8.
2. Binyamin Netanyahu in a speech to new immigrants to Israel.
3. Deuteronomy 30:3-6.
4. Isaiah 11:12.
5. Isaiah 43:5-6.
6. Jeremiah 24:6-7.
7. Jeremiah 31:10.
8. Ezekiel 11:16-20.
9. Amos 9:14-15.
10. Isaiah 49:14-16, 19-20.
11. Isaiah 62:1, 4-5.
12. Isaiah 62:6-7.
13. Isaiah 49:22.
14. Isaiah 60:9.
15. Matthew 25:34-40.
16. Deuteronomy 30:5-6.
17. Isaiah 51: 3, 11.
18. Isaiah 52:9.
19. Jeremiah 31:31-34.
20. Jeremiah 32:37-41.
21. Ezekiel 36:24-28.

22. Ezekiel 37:14.
23. Psalm 130:7-8.
24. Isaiah 59:20.
25. Isaiah 49:26.
26. Isaiah 62:11-12.
27. Luke 21:28.
28. Isaiah 60:1-3,14.
29. Jeremiah 3:17.
30. Isaiah 2:4.
31. Micah 4:6-7.
32. Zechariah 1:17; 8:3,7-8,23.
33. Deuteronomy 4:30-31.
34. Jeremiah 30:24.
35. Hosea 3:4-5.
36. Daniel 10:14.
37. Psalm 14:7.
38. Luke 21:24.
39. Psalm 102:18, 21-22.
40. Risto Santala, *The Messiah in the New Testament,* (Jerusalem: Keren Ahvah Meshihit, 1992), 239.
41. Matthew 24:32-35.
42. Ecclesiastes 3:1.

CHAPTER 11

1. Genesis 17:7-8.
2. Psalm 105:8-11.

3. Ezekiel 11:16-17.
4. Amos 9:14-15.
5. Jeremiah 16:14-15.
6. Jeremiah 31:10.
7. Luke 21:24.
8. Matthew 25:24-40.
9. Romans 15:27.
10. Bard, 26.
11. Walter K. Price, *Next Year in Jerusalem* (Chicago: Moody Press, 1975), 64-65.
12. Isaiah 51:3.

CHAPTER 12

1. Matthew 5:16.
2. Mark Twain, *The Innocents Abroad* (London: 1881), 441-442.
3. Section 14 Protection of Holy Places Law passed by the Israeli Knesset on June 27 under the heading entitled IV. Jerusalem and the Holy Places.
4. Tal, 173-175.
5. Tal, 157-160.
6. Tal, 94.
7. Congressional Record, March 25, 1975.
8. David Allen Lewis, *Israel and the USA: Restoring the Lost Pages of American History* (Springfield, MO: Menorah Press, 1993), 41-42.

9. *The New Encyclopedia Britannic Micropedia, Volume 8*, (Chicago: 1981), 817.
10. Lewis, 25-26.
11. Isaiah 62:1.
12. Micah 4:6-8.
13. Joel 3:1-2.

CHAPTER 13

1. Romans 11:18.
2. Matthew 28:18-20.
3. 1 John 3:18.
4. *The New York Times*, September 10, 2000.
5. Dr. Richard Booker.
6. Zechariah 14:16.
7. Zechariah 8:22.
8. Ezekiel 37:11-14.
9. Isaiah 49:22.
10. Isaiah 60:9.
11. Isaiah 40:1.
12. Matthew 25:34-40.
13. Romans 15:27.
14. 1 Chronicles 29:10-12.

BIBLIOGRAPHY

Al-Araby, Abdullah. *The Islamization of America*. Los Angeles: The Pen vs. The Sword, 2003.

Ankerberg, John and Weldon, John. *The Facts on Islam*. Eugene, OR: Harvest House Publishers, 1991.

Bard, Mitchell. *Myths and Facts: A Guide to the Arab-Israeli Conflict*. Chevy Chase, MD: American-Israeli Cooperative Enterprise, 2001.

Booker, Richard. *Islam, Christianity and Israel*. Houston: Sounds of the Trumpet, Inc., 1994.

Booker, Richard. *Why Christians Should Support Israel*. Houston: Sounds of the Trumpet, Inc., 2001.

Booker, Richard. *The Time to Favor Zion Has Come*. Houston: Sounds of the Trumpet, Inc., 1996.

Booker, Richard. *The Battle for Truth*. Houston: Sounds of the Trumpet, Inc., 2004.

Caner, Ergun and Emir. *Unveiling Islam*. Grand Rapids: Kregel Publications, 2002.

Cantrell, Ron. *The Mahdi: Hijacked Messiah*. Jerusalem, 2004.

Dixon, Murray. *Whose Promised Land?* Auckland, Australia: Heinemann Education, 1991.

Gold, Dore. *Hatred's Kingdom*. Washington, DC: Regnery Publishing, Inc., 2003.

Koranic references are from. *The Koran,* translated with notes by N.J. Dawood, New York: Penguin Books, 1993.

Lindsey, Hal. *The Everlasting Hatred: The Roots of Jihad.* Oracle House Publishing, 2002.

Morey, Robert. *The Islamic Invasion*. Eugene, OR: Harvest House Publishers, 1992.

Morey, Robert. *The Moon-god Allah in the Archeology of the Middle East*. Newport, PA: Research and Education Foundation, 1994.

Morey, Robert. *By Their Moles Ye Shall Know Them.* Newport, PA: Research and Education Foundation, 1995.

Morey, Robert. *Islam: The Religion of the Moon God*. Newport, PA: Research and Education Foundation, 1995.

Payne, Robert. *The History of Islam.* New York: Barnes and Noble, 1992.

Peck, Ron. *The Shadow of the Crescent*. Springfield, MO: Center for Ministry to Muslims.

Peters, Joan. *From Time Immemorial: The Origins of the Arab-Jewish Conflict Over Palestine.* New York: Harper and Row, Publishers, 1984.

Shorrosh, Anis. *Islam Revealed*. Nashville: Thomas Nelson, 1988.

Steyn, Mark. America Alone. Washington, DC: Regnery Publishing, Inc., 2006.

The Hadith Internet site: www.usc.edu/dept/MSA/reference/searchhadith.html.

About the Author

Richard Booker, MBA, PhD, is an ordained Christian minister, President of Sounds of the Trumpet, Inc., and the Founder/Director of the Institute for Hebraic-Christian Studies. Prior to entering the ministry, Richard had a successful business career. He is the author of 30 books and numerous seminars which are used by churches and Bible schools around the world.

Richard has traveled extensively for 30 years teaching in churches and at conferences on various aspects of the Christian life as well as Israel and the Hebraic roots of Christianity. He and his wife, Peggy, have lead yearly tour groups to Israel where, for 20 years, Richard has been a speaker at the International Christian Celebration of the Feast of Tabernacles in Jerusalem. This gathering is attended by 5,000 Christians from 100 nations.

Richard and Peggy co-founded the Institute for Hebraic-Christian Studies (IHCS) in 1997 as a ministry to educate Christians in the Hebraic culture and background of the Bible, build relationships between Christians and Jews, and give comfort and support to the people of Israel. Their tireless work on behalf of Christians and Jews has been recognized around the world as well as being represented at the Knesset Christian Allies Caucus.

Richard is considered a pioneer and spiritual father in teaching on Israel, Jewish-Christian relations, and the biblical Hebraic roots of Christianity. To learn more about his ministry, visit his Website and online bookstore at:

www.rbooker.com

or

www.soundsofthetrumpet.com.

To contact Dr. Booker about speaking at
your church or congregation, contact him at

shofarprb@aol.com.

Additional copies of this book and other book titles from DESTINY IMAGE are available at your local bookstore.

Call toll-free: 1-800-722-6774.

Send a request for a catalog to:

Destiny Image Publishers, Inc.

P.O. Box 310
Shippensburg, PA 17257-0310

"Speaking to the Purposes of God for this Generation and for the Generations to Come."

For a complete list of our titles, visit us at www.destinyimage.com